BE ALL YOU CAN BE

John C. Maxwell

Run So That You May Win
*i*victor.com

Victor Books is an imprint of Cook Communications Ministries,
Colorado Springs, Colorado 80918
Cook Communications, Paris, Ontario
Kingsway Communications, Eastbourne, England

Victor® is a registered trademark of Cook Communications
Ministries.

   10 11 12 13 14 Printing/Year 08 07 06 05 04 03 02

Recommended Dewey Decimal Classification: 301.155
Suggested Subject Heading: LEADERSHIP

ISBN: 1-56476-516-4

Library of Congress Cataloging-in-Publication Data

Maxwell, John C., 1947-
      Be all you can be / John C. Maxwell.
         p. cm.
      Originally published: c1987
      ISBN 1-56476-516-4
      1. Success—Religious aspects—Christianity.   I. Title.
   BV4598.3 .M39 2002
   248.4—dc21
2001005367

BE ALL YOU CAN BE!

is dedicated to the hundreds of men and women who belong to my Injoy Life Club. These people strive to reach their potential for the glory of God. It is my joy to journey with them!

CONTENTS

ACKNOWLEDGEMENTS

This book is the product of leadership lessons I gave to the staff at Skyline Wesleyan Church. Each month, these lessons are taped and then sent to the thousands of men and women throughout the world who subscribe to the INJOY Life Club.

My special thanks go to Barbara Babby, who edited this book, and to Barbara Brumagin, who coordinated the project.

A continual thanks goes to my family, Margaret, Elizabeth, and Joel, who are always supportive of my ministry.

If you would like more information about the monthly lessons offered through the INJOY Life Club, our you would like a free catalog of the audio, video, and written materials created by John Maxwell, please write INJOY, 1530 Jamacha Road, Suite D, El Cajon, CA 92109. Or call (800) 333-6506.

FOREWORD

Exciting, informative, directional, and extremely helpful are just some of the words to describe <u>Be All You Can Be</u>! Dr. John Maxwell is truly one of the most effective and compassionate "word merchants" of the 20th century. He writes from a considerable intellect but, more importantly, he writes from his heart. This is what all effective communicators do. As Dr. Maxwell says, "If there is no faith in the future, there is no power in the present." The beautiful thing about <u>Be All You Can Be</u>! is the fact that it gives the reader considerable hope for the future which obviously is going to give him a great deal of power in the present. This enables each of us to be more effective today, which means our tomorrows have to be better.

<u>Be All You Can Be</u>! can be beautiful in three different ways. You can pick it up for the momentary lift in spirits by reading a page or two. You can feast more bountifully from the banquet table of great thoughts and ideas and really get some instructional lifts which will make a difference. Or you can nourish yourself on a regular basis with the gems of wisdom which prevail throughout the book. It's clear and concise so that you never wonder what is means. In a nutshell, it challenges us to be all that we can be and then gives us some clear-cut guidelines to accomplish that objective. It's good—very good.

Zig Ziglar

YES, YOU CAN!

I've always tried to turn problem situations into opportunities for creative alternatives. On a warm day some time ago my wife, Margaret, and I were traveling in a rural part of Ohio, and we were thirsty. The fast food restaurant where we stopped had ice but no diet Coke. My solution was to obtain a cup of ice and buy a can of diet Coke at a nearby store. It seemed easy enough to me when I made my request, but the counter girl said with great conviction, "I'm sorry, I can't do that." No doubt she had a "no, I can't" mind-set that needed to be reprogrammed.

I looked back at her, smiled, and said, "Yes, you can!" Her face brightened and she replied, "OK!" With a positive and eager response she produced a cup of ice. That's all it took—my permission for her to respond to a creative alternative.

All she needed was somebody to say, "yes, you can." What I want this book to do is to give you that "Yes, you can" spirit in your life.

The second thing I want this book to do is to give you some success principles that really work. You see, there are principles of success and there are principles of failure. There is a simple process of applying these success principles. It involves four steps: know, show, go, and grow. You have to know the principles first of all, and then you have to show them. We're to model these principles in front of others, since people have to see them. That's more important even than hearing the principles. The going is the experience. You have to roll up your sleeves, get out into the field, and experience them. As you grow, assess yourself. Ask yourself, How am I doing? Are these principles really taking hold of my life? Is it like breathing? Is it becoming natural to me? I want to share principles that will help you grow—in your own Christian life and in your leadership.

Third, I want to provide tools for people in leadership positions. When I speak of tools, I'm speaking of information. Information is power, and every person has influence; that's what leadership is, and the more information we have, the more power we'll have in leading others. The more information we can impart to others, the more we can influence others in a positive way.

I want you to take the material that I give you and pass it on to others. It's not any good if it's just assimilated for yourself. It must be passed on.

The fourth goal for Be All You Can Be is to help develop Christian leaders who will make a difference. I'm interested in challenging you. If we are unchallenged, we are unchanged. Do you know the difference between leaders, followers, and losers? Leaders stretch with challenges. Followers struggle with challenges. Losers shrink from challenges. I want you to stretch with this material. I want you to be like a rubber band—it's not useful until it's stretched.

The last goal I have for this book is to help you develop healthy, joyful attitudes. You see, most of our problems are in our heads. It's not what happens to us; it's what happens in us. Joy is a by-product of following right principles.

As I was reading John 15 on a plane a few months ago, I came across Jesus' words in verse 11, "These things I have spoken to you that My joy may be in you and that your joy may be made full." Those words leaped out at me, and I began to realize that Jesus was talking to His disciples, to Christians, and He was basically saying that even though they had been with Him for three years, there was a possibility that they would not have continual joy in their lives. He was telling them that joy and happiness become real only as we put the right principles into practice. What I share with you in this book I share because I want to help you be a fruitful, joyful Christian.

Chapter One

FRUITFULNESS IS FUN!

In John 15, Jesus says that fruitfulness is fun. In fact, the theme of John 15 is that Jesus wants us to live fruitful lives. Look at verse 16: "You did not choose Me, but I chose you, and appointed you, that you should go and bear fruit, and that your fruit should remain, that whatever you ask of the Father in My name, He may give it to you."

Let me share with you what I consider to be fruitfulness according to the Bible. When God speaks in His Word of a fruitful life, He means active, positive attitudes. The passage of Scripture that deals with the fruit of the spirit, Galatians 5:22-23, is the premier passage on fruitful living. "The fruit of the Spirit is love, joy, peace, patience, kindness, goodness, faithfulness, gentleness, self-control; against such things there is no law." Fruitfulness is exhibiting positive, active attitudes on a daily basis in our lives. When that happens, we begin to sense real joy and to see positive things happen in our lives. When we put these attitudes together, five "PRs" must appear.

First of all, there are positive results. When you begin to inject these attitudes into your society, you're going to see constructive results. You're going to have positive relationships. You will begin to develop fruitful relationships with others.

You're going to have positive reactions, especially in areas that were previously tough problem areas for you. You're going to find that you receive reactions that are positive when you begin to have these active, positive attitudes.

You'll receive positive reinforcement. Life is like a mirror; what you show is what you see; what you put in is what you get out. When you encourage others, you'll find that they will encourage you. Attitudes are contagious.

Last, you'll have positive rejoicing. That's what Jesus says in John 15:11. "These things I have spoken to you, that My joy may be in you, and that your joy may be made full." People often tell me they're not happy; they say they're unfulfilled. They talk about not having joy in their lives. I get the impression that seeking for joy has become their purpose in life—but joy (or happiness or fulfillment) comes to us not when we seek it, but when we put the right principles into practice in our lives. It is a by-product of doing what is right.

It is when we live by the right principles that we begin to love the right principles. Most of the time, we want to love first. We want to fall in love with what is right and then have it happen to us. That's backward—it's when we learn what's right and live according to it that we begin to want to be right; then we begin to have the by-product, which is joy. You have probably seen the bumper sticker that asks, "Are we having fun yet?" Every time I see that bumper sticker, I want to write another one: "Are we doing right yet?" If we're doing right, we'll be having fun.

Our Power Source

In John 15:1-10, Jesus gives us the principles of fruitful living. Let's look at them together. First, our potential for fruitful living is unlimited because of our source. Jesus starts by saying, "I am the true vine" (v. 1). Jesus is our source. When we realize that, then we understand why Paul could say, "I can do all things through Christ who strengthens me" (Phil. 4:13). We become fruitful when we tap into the right source.

A friend of mine was discussing the implications of Micah 6:8 with his seven-year-old grandson: "What does the Lord require of you but to do justice, to love kindness, and to walk humbly with your God?" The little boy, who was memorizing this verse, said, "Grandpa, it's hard to be humble if you're really walking with God." That's great theology coming from a seven-year-old. When we begin to get a glimpse of the unlimited resources at our disposal—the power of God Himself—then and only then will we sense the assurance that we are fully equipped to do whatever it is that God calls us to do.

We might feel like the little mouse who was crossing a bridge over a very deep ravine with an elephant. As the elephant and the mouse crossed the bridge, the bridge shook. When they got to the other side, the mouse looked at his huge companion and said, "Boy, we really shook that bridge, didn't we?"

When we walk with God, that's often how we feel—like a mouse with the strength of an elephant. After crossing life's troubled waters, we can say with the mouse, "God, we really shook that bridge, didn't we?"

Hudson Taylor, the great missionary to China, said,

"Many Christians estimate difficulty in the light of their own resources, and thus they attempt very little, and they always fail. All giants have been weak men who did great things for God because they reckoned on His power and His presence to be with them."

Like David, who said, "The battle is the Lord's" (1 Sam. 17:47), we also need to understand that Jesus is our source, and we can be directly connected to Him.

The Care of Our Owner

In this passage of Scripture, Jesus says that we have potential for fruitful living not only because of our source but because of our care. Just as Jesus is the source, the Father is the vinedresser. The vinedresser takes care of the vine; he would be a man of skill and knowledge, an expert at growing grapes. But in this passage of Scripture, He is also the owner. When you think of an owner, you think of personal interest. You think of commitment—something more than knowledge and skill. As branches we not only have our source from the vine, but we have God who oversees us, takes cares of us, and prepares us to be productive and fruitful.

You've probably noticed that the person who owns something, whatever it is, has a certain pride that a mere observer never has. I remember when I was a little kid, my grandfather often walked me around his farm. As we walked and looked, he would find uniqueness and beauty in things I wouldn't have looked at twice. He would see great potential in a rundown shed on a back lot; I would see kindling. He would show me a rusty, old tractor and see a machine with possibilities; I would see a piece of rust-covered junk. Why? How could we look at the same objects and see different things? He owned them and I didn't. Ownership makes a difference. God owns us, so when He looks at our lives, He looks at them not as an observer but as an investor.

Our Purging

Our potential for fruitful living is great because Jesus is our source. The fact that God is our caretaker and owner adds to that potential. One of the things God does as vinedresser is to purge us. His purging greatly increases our potential for fruitful living. "Every branch that bears fruit, He prunes it, that it may bear more fruit" (v. 2). God, the vinedresser, removes everything that hinders our usefulness. He knows that if He doesn't cut back the deadwood, all of our resources will to toward producing more wood and we won't be fruit producers.

I have found that productive people are continually being pruned, going through this process that God uses to make us more fruitful. And God knows exactly what to prune from our lives. He's like the professional logger, who, when there's a jam on the river, climbs a tall tree, looks over all the logs, and identifies the problem area. Then he takes a little bit of dynamite and blows that part up so the logs can continue to flow down river. Now, that's not the way I'd do it. I would probably jump in and start knocking logs around until I finally worked my way to the problem area. But God doesn't mess around with peripherals. He goes right in with His dynamite and blows up only the areas in our lives that aren't productive. He cuts away that "sin which so easily entangles us" (Heb. 12:1), whatever it is that keeps us from becoming the persons we really want to become.

Our Partnership

Our potential for fruitfulness is also tremendous because of our partnership. In verse 4, Jesus talks about this partnership. (And in fact, you can see it throughout the passage.) "Abide in Me, and I in you. As the branch cannot bear fruit of itself, unless it abides in the vine, so neither can you, unless you abide in Me." Ten times in verses 4-10 we see the word *abide*. Basically He's saying, "Connect with the vine, and everything will be fine." When Robert Morrison was on the way to China, where he would be a missionary, the captain of the ship was skeptical of his dream and gave him a hard time. As Morrison was leaving the ship, the captain said to him, "I suppose you think you're going to make an impression on China." Robert Morrison replied simply, "No sir. I believe God will." He was in partnership with God.

This partnership with God ought to give us the same sense of confidence as the youngster had who was selling five-cent pencils door-to-door to raise money for a 30-million-dollar hospital for the community. One day a woman opened the door, and he said, "Ma'am, would you buy one or two pencils from me? I'm going to help build a 30-million-dollar hospital for our community." She said, "Sonny, that's a mighty big goal for just one kid selling pencils for a nickel." He said, "Oh, Ma'am, it's not me alone. See that boy across the street? He's my partner. He's helping. We're really doing it together." This little boy had great faith in a partner who was probably his equal. Should we not have this kind of confidence in a God who is unequaled, a God who is in partnership with us to make our lives fruitful?

Our Promise

We also have potential for fruitfulness because of the promise given to us in verse 7. "If you abide in Me, and My words abide in you, ask whatever you wish, and it shall be done for you." There are two observations I would like to make. First, the promise is conditional: if we abide in Him. Second, our asking needs to be according to His Word. What Jesus is really saying is that if we abide in Him, our delight will be in Him, so much so that we will ask all things according to His will. It reminds me of Psalm 37:4: "Delight yourself in the Lord; and He will give you the desires of your heart." Delight comes before desire. If I delight, what I delight in determines what I desire. If I delight in God, my desire will be to do things according to His will and to ask according to His will. Too often we try to make this principle work in reverse.

As a high school student, one of my chores was to do the dinner dishes. I hated doing the dishes. I was dating Margaret at the time, and often the prospect of seeing her in the evening outweighed my sense of duty at home, so I would jump in the car and be gone before I was missed. When I got to her house, you can guess what she was doing! I would immediately pick up a towel and begin drying dishes—and have a wonderful time doing it! The person I delighted in was doing dishes, and when you really delight in someone, you enjoy doing things you normally dislike. So often we lack desire because our delight is not great enough. God promises us that if we delight in Him, we will desire things we need, and He will give them to us.

Our Life's Purpose

Our potential for fruitfulness is great because of the purpose in our lives. That's in verse 8: "By this is My Father glorified, that you bear much fruit, and so prove to be My disciples." In other words, we are created to be fruitful. That's our purpose. Look at verse 16: "You did not choose Me, but I chose you, and appointed you." Why? "That you should go and bear fruit," that you should have active, positive attitudes in your life. We have been chosen, appointed by God, for fruitful living. Those active, positive attitudes, like love, joy, peace, and long-suffering, ought to be becoming part of our lives. When they become part of us inwardly, then we begin to pass them on.

The problem so often with us Christians is that we do not show these positive attitudes that can make us salt and light in our world. The story is told that when Berlin was being divided into East Berlin, controlled by the Communists, and West Berlin, part of the free world, a group of East Berliners dumped a whole truck-load of garbage on the west side. The people from West Berlin thought they'd pick up all the garbage, put it on a truck, and dump if back on the east side. Then they decided that wasn't the way to handle it. Instead they filled a dump truck with canned goods and other non-perishable food items, went over to the east side, stacked it neatly, and put a sign beside it. The sign read, "Each gives what each has to give." I think they were preaching, don't you? You can only give fruit to others when you are living a fruitful life inwardly.

The Fruit of Obedience

Our potential for fruitfulness is tremendous because of our obedience. Jesus says in verses 7 and 10 that if we abide in Him and if we keep His commandments, we will be fruitful. I think the key word is that little *if.* I have a mug at home that says, "If it's to be, it's up to me." I think that's what Jesus is saying. He says if you're going to be fruitful, it going to be up to you. Jesus assumes in John 15 that He will have a fruitful relationship with us. In verse 6 He says, "If anyone does not abide in Me." He doesn't say, "If I do not abide in you." He's going to be plugged into us. His question for us is, Are you going to be plugged into Me? He's already here; He has the power; He has the strength; He has the wisdom to implant in us; He has all the resources that we need, and He's ready to deliver. All we need to do is to plug into Him.

Why don't we always abide in Him? Pure lack of obedience. We begin to think that we can do it on our own; we begin to have an unhealthy self-confidence instead of a Christ-confidence. When we do not have active, positive attitudes, it is because we aren't plugged into the vine. Christians should not have to psych themselves up every day, as the world does, to have active, positive attitudes. It will be as natural as breathing when the relationship is right. Jesus is saying that when the relationship is right, we begin to live fruitful lives. That's when we really begin to become productive.

Everybody wants to be productive. A psychologist at Stanford University tried to show that we live for productive results, or fruit. This researcher hired a man—a logger. He said, "I'll pay you double what you get paid in the logging camp, if you'll take the blunt end of this axe and just pound this log all day. You never have to cut one piece of wood. Just take the end that is blunt and hit it as hard as you can, just as you would if you were logging." The man worked for half a day and he quit. The psychologist asked, "Why did you quit?" The logger said, "Because every time I move an ax, I have to see the chips fly. If I don't see the chips fly, it's no fun." I'm convinced that there are many Christians who are using the wrong end of their axes, and there are no chips flying. In other words, they are producing no fruit, and their joy is gone. Joy has been replaced by a sense of futility, uselessness, immobility. Fruitful people like to see the chips fly.

Formula for Fruitfulness

Jesus gives us a three-word formula for fruitfulness in John 15. These three words are the ones I want you to remember, because they are the key to fruitful living. The first word is *remain*. Throughout John 15 Jesus tells us to remain. In fact, the word *abide* in the original language can be translated "remain." "Remain in Me," Jesus says. He's talking about our willingness to take time with Him in prayer and in study of the Word. We need to let Him begin to be part of our lives and work on our lives.

The second word in the formula is *receive*. Jesus says in John 15 that if we remain in Him, we will begin to receive certain things. What we'll receive is good, fruitful living.

The third word is reproduce. If we remain in Him, we're going to receive what He has for us, then and only then will we begin to reproduce in our lives.

Fruitful Follow-Up

Let me give you a couple of suggestions for applying these things to your life. First of all, I would encourage you to commit yourself *now* to a productive lifestyle. Climb out on the limb; that's where the fruit is. All great accomplishments have to begin with an initial decision. Make up your mind that you're going to be a fruitful Christian, that you're going to begin to reproduce for Christ.

Second, follow the formula for fruitfulness I just gave you, and follow it daily. *Remain* by spending perhaps fifteen minutes in prayer and meditation daily. *Receive* by spending thirty minutes every day in the Word of God, positive books, and teaching tapes. Feed your mind on things that will help you think right and then reproduce. Find someone—today, not tomorrow—with whom you can share maybe one of the truths you learned from this chapter. Pass it on. One of the quickest ways to grow is to tell someone else what you just learned. The more you verbalize it, the more it becomes ingrained in your life.

Third, list the seeds that you are planting in your life. What things are you doing right now that are going to help you to be fruitful? Think not only of today but also of a year from now and five years from now. What are you investing in the soil of your life that's going to come back to you tenfold, thirtyfold, or a hundredfold?

Fourth, list some positive results that are happening in your life. If you're connected to the vine, you should be seeing evidences of that relationship. Remember the five "PRs"? They should begin to happen in your life. Look for them. Write them down and carry them with you.

As you begin to put good seed into the soil of your life, you should be starting to reap some positive benefits, possibly in and through people who have previously reacted negatively. Begin to cultivate the soil; plant some positive seeds and watch the five "PRs" come back to you. Remember the theme: "These things I have spoken to you, that My joy may be in you, and that your joy may be made full" (John 15:11).

Chapter Two

FORMULA FOR
SUCCESS

I recently heard a story about a man who was honored as his city's leading citizen. Called on to tell the story of his life, he said, "Friends and neighbors, when I first came here 30 years ago, I walked into your town on a muddy dirt road with only the suit on my back, the shoes on my feet, and all of my earthly possessions wrapped up in a red bandanna tied to a stick, which I carried over my shoulder. Today I'm the chairman of the board of the bank. I own hotels, apartment buildings, office buildings, three companies with branches in 49 cities, and I am on the boards of all the leading clubs. Yes, friends, your city has been very good to me."

After the banquet a youngster approached the great an and asked him, "Sir, could you tell me what you wrapped in that red bandanna when you walked into this town 30 years ago?" The man said, "I think son, it was about a half million dollars in cash and $900,000 in government bonds."

For us to understand what success is, we have to first ask what's in the red bandanna. If I asked you to define what success is, you would define it according to what you have wrapped up in your red bandanna, the things you really need in order to live.

What Is Success?

I want to approach this formula for success from two angles. First we need to define success from the world's point of view, and then we need to define success from a Christian perspective. There is a difference.

The best way to define success from the world's standpoint is that it's the power with which to acquire whatever one demands of life without violating the rights of others. In other words, it's the power to get what you want without stepping on other people: worldly success equals power. But a Christian definition of success has to include more than that. Here's my definition of success: choosing to enter into the arena of action, determined to give yourself to that cause which will better mankind and last for eternity. Success is more than just power or not violating the rights of others; it is the privilege of contributing to the betterment of others.

According to the world's definition of success, self demands of life, whereas according to the Christian definition of success, life demands of self. The world can say that I am successful as long as I meet my needs even if I do not help others. The Christian has to say that to be a success, I must contribute to the welfare of others. To put it another way, to be all I can be, I need to help you be all you can be.

The only one who can stop you from becoming the person God intends you to be is you. If you're not the person God had in mind when He created you, it's not His fault. He never asks us to be what He doesn't enable us to be. But too many times we stop short—we never attain success.

Why Do People Fail?

I think there area three reasons why people do not become successful.

Many people just don't feel the need to succeed. These people are secure; they don't need to prove anything. They're happy, content, and they like what's happening to them. But if success means becoming all that God intends us to be, and we're satisfied with less than that, we not only fall short of God's glory ourselves but we limit what others can be for Him.

The greatest responsibility of leaders is that they not shortchange themselves, thereby shortchanging those whom they lead. If God has given a gift, we are to use it and succeed, so that we not only enhance the kingdom from our perspective but from our followers' as well.

The second reason people do not succeed is that *they are afraid of success.* What are some of the reasons people fear success? Sometimes we are afraid because success puts pressure on us to continue to succeed. A person who gets straight A's on a report card sets a pattern of achievement and must keep achieving. Often we just don't want to be responsible, so we shrink from success.

People who have poor self-images will always shy away from success. Others don't want to be successful because they don't like to be lonely. They would rather be with the crowd; it's lonely at the top. Risk is another reason; people don't want to stick their necks out.

There are many more reasons, but the main point is that some people are afraid of success.

The third reason why many people fail is that they are suspicious of success. It's as if they think that if you want to be successful, you certainly can't be spiritual: successful people can't be humble. We've almost equated humility with poverty. Yet when I look through the Word of God, one of the things that impresses me most is that the Bible is chock-full of successful people who chose to enter into the arena of action and give themselves to a cause that would better humanity. They were successful in changing lives for eternity. Think of people like Joseph, Nehemiah, the Apostle Paul, Joshua, David, and Abraham. Many of the men of the Bible were what we would consider to be successful. To fail to become all that God created you to become limits not only yourself but also those under your influence.

S—Select Your Goal

Let's take each letter of the word success and make an acrostic. The first letter S stands for "select your goal." The reason most people don't succeed is simply that they really don't know what they want out of life. The Apostle Paul wrote, "One thing I do" (Phil. 3:13). He knew what he wanted to do. I heard a fellow say one time that success is the "progressive realization of a pre-determined, worthwhile goal." We have to know where we are going.

The goal is predetermined. Success is not an accident; it's not luck or fate. It is predetermined. *Success is worthwhile.* Nothing is successful that does not contribute in a positive way to help people. *Success is continual.* It's not an event but a journey, an ongoing process. It's not an accolade that we receive for a race won or a job well-done. Success is the positive result of steady forward movement.

Research shows that approximately 95 percent of us have never written out our goals in life, but of the 5 percent who have, 95 percent have achieved their goals. In 1953 at Yale University, 3 percent of the graduating class had specific, written goals for their lives. In 1975 researchers found that the 3 percent who wrote down their goals had accomplished more than the other 97 percent put together.

I wonder how much we don't achieve because we don't establish definite goals and put them in writing. I run into people all the time who don't set definite goals because there are too many factors in life over which they have no control. There are physical limits to what we can do. I can only throw a ball so high and so far— beyond that maximum I have no control. But within the limit of my ability I have total freedom. Determinism and free will are both a part of life, but it is better to make the most of what we can do than to bemoan what we cannot do.

The average person's lifetime includes 20 years of sleeping, 6 years of watching television, 5 years of dressing and shaving, 3 years of waiting for others, 1 year on the telephone, and 4 months of tying shoes. To help you understand the importance of goals and to facilitate your own goal- setting, let me give you six important guidelines.

Your goal must include others. No goal is worthwhile that is only for yourself. Set a goal big enough to include and help other people.

Your goal must be worthwhile. There is no such thing as a successful frivolous goal.

Your goal must be clean. If you don't know where you are headed, a map will be of no use.

Your goal must be measurable. You need a way to see if you are making any progress toward the goal.

Your goal must be expandable. Don't set your goals in concrete. If your goal is not expandable, it's expendable. As we grow, we see the picture more clearly, and we need to continually "up" our goals. It's a sad day when we realize we have achieved our goals and have nothing else to do.

Your goals must be filled with conviction. Conviction is the unshaken confidence that the goal is worthwhile. It's the fuel that pushes us to achieve.

U—Unlock Your Imprisoned Potential

Most people only use about 10 percent of their potential; if they use as much as 25 percent, they're called geniuses. If we can go from using 10 percent of our potential to using 20 percent, we could double our productivity and still have 80 percent of our potential untapped.

Michelangelo worked on 44 statues in his life. He only complete 14 of them. *David* and *Moses* are probably the most famous. The other ones were never finished. They're just blocks of stone, with perhaps an arm or a head. There is a museum in Italy where you can see these unfinished works, the unfulfilled potential of a great genius.

It is sad enough to realize that there are unfinished works of Michelangelo, but what is even more sad is to look every day at the people around us and realize that they are like blocks of stone that haven't yet been developed. If we as leaders could somehow, through the wisdom and the power of God, take the chisel to our people—not the ball bat, the chisel—and begin to peck away, define what they are, and begin to release them from that granite block that has kept them from being what they should be, then we would be doing our people a great service.

How do you unlock your potential? Here are just a few ways to begin.

Look up. The first thing is to look up and find a model, somebody who is doing a better job than you are. Are there any people that you know who are reaching more of their potential now than ever before because they know you? Can you think of anything better as a parent, an employer, or a pastor to do for others than to help unlock their potential by being a model for them?

Nothing can be more challenging than to be the person whom others look up to.

What we need is somebody a little bigger and a little better than we are, and we need to spend time with them. Let me give you an example. I play racquetball with a colleague of mine. He is a good racquetball player; in fact he is better than I am, and he always wins the first game. I'm challenged because he's better than I am, so I give it my best. If you have ever played anybody who is worse than you, you know that you start going downhill. You get lazy, and you don't keep your mind on the game. That's what happens to my colleague. By the third game, I win. When you play somebody better, you stretch; when you play somebody worse, you shrink.

So if you want to unlock your hidden potential, spend your time with people who will stretch you. Find somebody who thinks faster, runs faster, and aims higher. Those are the people who will lift you up.

Give Up. To reach your potential, we must give up at any moment all that we are in order to receive what we can become. Many people don't understand this. They want to hang on to what they are and at the same time be all they can be. You have to let go.

In the Bible there are all kinds of beautiful illustrations of men of God who gave up something to rise higher. Abraham gave up his home to seek a better country. Moses gave up the riches of Egypt. David gave up security. John the Baptist gave up being first so he could be second. The Apostle Paul have up his past and made a radical turnaround. Jesus Himself gave up His rights. And you will find that you too will have to give up something good if you want something better.

You'll never find anybody who achieves great success in life without a give-up story. Nothing comes free.

Fire up. I'm talking about what Phillips Brooks meant when he said, "Sad is the day for any man when he becomes absolutely satisfied with the life that he is living, the thoughts he is thinking and the deeds he is doing; until there ceases to be forever beating at the door of his soul a desire to do something larger which he seeks and knows he was meant and intended to do."

Show up. Nothing will help you reach your potential like facing the challenges of your life. Some people never become all they can be because when they see a challenge coming, they fail to show up for the match. They close the door and hide in the corner while the challenge is met by someone else. Don't be intimidated by challenges: meet them head-on.

Go up. If we look up to a person who is reaching his or her potential, if we give up anything that hinders us from being our best, if we fire up our desires until we are no longer satisfied, and if we show up to our challenges and not become fearful, then we will go up. We'll go up to the top of our potential—but only after we look up, give up, fire up, and show up.

C—Commit Yourself to God's Plan

Ted Engstrom said, "Success means a person is reaching the maximum potential available to him at any given moment."

If success is what Ted Engstrom says it is—tapping into the available potential that we have and making these best use of it—shouldn't Christians be more successful than non-Christians? The power God gives to Spirit-filled believers ought to make a world of difference between them and non believers. "Greater is He who is in you than he who is in the world" (1 John 4:4). "I can do all things through Him who strengthens me" (Phil. 4:13). We have all these things through the power of God's Spirit that should enable us to live on a higher plane.

How do I find God's plan for my life? How do I commit myself to God's plan? There are seven questions to ask yourself.

> • *Am I consecrated to Him?* Romans 12:1-2 tells us that we have to be consecrated before we can know the plan of God.

> • *Am I spending time with Him?* I find God's plan when I spend time getting to know God. The more intimate I become with God, the more knowledgeable I become about His plan for my life.

• *What are my gifts?* Most of the time the plan of God fits right in with the gifts God has given me.

• *What are my desires?* I have found that my desires and gifts also fit together. The gifts God gives us are often realized through our desires.

• *What are my Christian friends saying?* What do they say are my strengths and weaknesses?

• *What are my opportunities?* What lies before me that God may be giving to me as an open door to walk through?

• *Am I in ministry now?* It's amazing how many people who want to know God's plan for their lives are doing nothing now. If you really want to know what God's plan is for your life, do something. God works through a busy person.

Commit yourself to God's plan.

C—Chart Your Course

This has to do with planning. It's better to look ahead and prepare than look back and regret.

A passenger was talking to the captain of the Queen Mary during an ocean cruise, and he asked the captain, "How long would it take you before you could stop this vessel?" The captain said, "If I shut down all the engines, it would take me a little over a mile to get this vessel completely stopped." He added, "A good captain thinks at least a mile ahead."

I went through the Proverbs in the Living Bible, and here are the verses I pulled out that have to do with planning.

We should make plans—counting on God to direct us. (Prov. 16:9)

Plans go wrong with too few counselors; many counselors   bring success. (Prov. 15:22)

It is dangerous and sinful to rush into the unknown. (Prov. 19:2)

A sensible man watches for problems and prepares to meet them. The simpleton never looks, and suffers the consequences. (Prov. 27:12)]

Any enterprise is built by wise planning, becomes strong through common sense, and profits wonderfully by keeping abreast of the facts. (Prov. 24:3-4)

Plan ahead, chart your course, and if God is going to be your partner, make your plans large.

E—Expect Problems

Paul Harvey said, "You can always tell when you are on the road to success; it's uphill all the way." If you find a path that has no problems, you will find that it leads nowhere.

I've talked many times to leaders about "sap strata." Sap strata are those levels of living beyond which it is hard to rise. It happens in churches, organizations, and in individual lives. Have you ever felt that you just weren't making any progress, as if you were hitting your head up against the wall? We have to make an extra burst of effort to get through those strata that keep us from being what God wants us to become. There are two ways to meet our problems, two ways to get through those sap strata. One way is to *change the problem*. This in only a temporary, partial solution. We can try to make the problem more manageable, but it will get out of hand again tomorrow.

The most effective way for us to overcome our problems is to change the person. Adversity is not our greatest enemy. The human spirit is capable of great resiliency and resourcefulness in the face of hardship. It's not problems that mess us up. Someone said, "Cripple [a man] and you have Sir Walter Scott. Lock him in prison and you have John Bunyan. Bury him in the snows of Valley Forge and you have George Washington. Raise him in poverty and you have Abraham Lincoln. Strike him down with infantile paralysis and he becomes Franklin Delano Roosevelt. Burn him so severely that doctors say he will never walk again and you have Glen Cunningham, who set the world's record in 1934 for the one-minute mile. Deafen him and you'll have Ludwig van Beethoven. Call him a slow learner, retarded, and write him off as uneducatable and you have Albert Einstein."

S—Stand Firm on Your Commitment

The word of God encourages us in 1 Corinthians 15:58, "Be steadfast, immovable, always abounding in the work of the Lord, knowing that your toil is not in vain in the Lord." Someone asked James Corbett, the heavyweight boxing champion at one time, what it took to be a heavyweight champion, and he said, "Fight one more round." When asked how he had been so successful in his inventions, Thomas Edison said, "I start where other men leave off." Napoleon Hill, in his book Think and Grow Rich, records that he studied 500 of the wealthiest men in the world and concluded that all wealthy men are persistent. When Winston Churchill went back to his alma mater to speak, the audience anticipated a great speech from the prime minister. He stood before them and said six words: "Never, never, never, never give up." That was it; the speech was over. And that is probably the speech for which he is most remembered. Stand firm on your commitment. Don't be a quitter.

S—Surrender Everything to Jesus Christ

Don't ever forget that although you may succeed beyond your fondest hopes and your greatest expectations, you will never succeed beyond the purpose to which you are willing to surrender. Seek first the kingdom of God and His righteousness and all of these other things shall be added unto you (Matt. 6:33).

The secret of the surrendered life is giving God the first part of every day, the first day of every week, the first portion of your income, the first consideration in every decision, and the first place in all of your life. When we surrender to Him, then we have a power that really caps off the formula for success. Surrender is what brings power. We fight for power and we lose it; we surrender and we find it.

Jesus Christ has not only shown us the righteous life—many great and good men and women did that before His time—but He has given us the power to live this righteous life. He not only shows us the beauty of God, as others have done, but He gives us the means by which we can become part of that beauty. We can learn the power of hourly surrender to the living Christ. Change in our lives is not brought about by our tense tinkering. It is brought about by the radiant, immeasurable energy of Christ, which has never left the world since He first said yes to God. His yes was complete; He kept nothing back for Himself.

As Flora Slosson Wuellner says, "There is nothing so tragically ineffectual as trying to live the Christian life without the Christian power. Try turning the other cheek without using the spiritual weapons of Christ's power to love and see what destructive situation develops. Try going the second mile with a neighbor without going all the way to surrender to Christ and see the damage done to the neighbor's personality and your own.

Try to love and pray unceasingly without turning daily to the living water of Christ and see how quickly the personal well runs dry." Surrender to Jesus Christ.

Success is a word that is greatly misunderstood, and we need to grasp what it means biblically to be a success—to love God with all of our heart, our mind, our soul, and our strength; to allow Him to unlock the imprisoned potential in our lives; to set godly goals and not be content to settle for second best when we realize that God gave everything He could give so that we could have the very best of life; and to realize that one of the greatest sins we commit against God is not reaching the potential He has placed in us.

Chapter Three

STRETCH TO SUCCESS

Rubber bands come in different sizes and different colors and different shapes, but they all work on the same principle: they must be stretched to be effective. Like rubber bands, our personalities, talents, and gifts are different; we're also not effective unless we're stretched. If you're not stretching in your own personal walk with God and in your leadership abilities, then you're not going to be able to be as effective for God as your really need to be.

Leonard Ravenhill relates that a group of tourists were in a village in Europe, and one of them asked an elderly villager, "Have any great men been born in this village?" The old man replied, "Nope, only babies." Every person who has ever achieved anything has stretched for it. There's no such thing as a self-made person; there's no such thing as a person who comes into the world fully equipped for success. Every person who has ever made it to the top, every person who has achieved anything for God, every person who has been effective has learned to stretch.

One of the most common mistakes, and one of the costliest, is thinking that success is due to some genius, some magic something or other, which we do not possess.

Success is due to our stretching to the challenges of life. Failure comes when we shrink from them. There's no such think as a man who was born great.

Why Don't We Stretch?

I would guess that 95 percent of us try to avoid stretching. When we come up against something that is bigger than we are, we tend to back off. What keeps us from expanding? Why do we avoid these stretching experiences.

Fear has to be the number-one reason. The unknown out there can really paralyze us. Another reason is that we're *satisfied*. Why stretch? We already like where we are; we have it made. Or perhaps there's a streak of *laziness* in us. There are times when we would just rather take it easy. I have found that *self-esteem* has a lot to do with one's willingness to stretch. A lot of people with low self-esteem have above average ability; they just do not see themselves in the proper light. Some of us just don't want to be *different*. If you stretch, you're no longer ordinary. To stretch is to be out of sync with many of our friends and associates.

I would encourage you to put this book down for a moment and evaluate yourself. Ask yourself why it is that you're not always stretching.

Take about five minutes to do some introspection and be honest as you sense God dealing with the reasons for your complacency. If you're trying to avoid stretching, you need to begin to regroup so you can become useful and effective in your ministry and leadership.

Motivated to Stretch

Most of us need to be motivated before we will stretch. It's not something that comes naturally. We need to learn how to stretch and motivate ourselves, but we also need to know how to motivate others and help them to reach their potential.

One of my modern-day heroes is Bear Bryant, who was the coach for the Alabama Crimson Tide for many years and who held the record for several years as the college football coach with the most victories. Bear Bryant was an outstanding coach and a tremendous motivator. His players knew they had better play good football. The story is told that during one important game his team was ahead by six points with only a minute left in the game, and they had the ball. It looked as if they had the game sewed up. He sent in a running play to his quarterback, but the quarterback decided to surprise the other team—and Coach Bryant—by calling a pass play. He said, "They're looking for the run; let's throw a pass." So he went back and threw a pass, and sure enough, the defensive cornerback, who was the speed champion of the league, intercepted the ball and headed toward the goal line. Alabama was about to lose the game. The Alabama quarterback, who was known for a good arm but not for fast legs, took off after the cornerback and caught him on the five-yard line. He saved the game; Alabama won. The opposing coach went to Bear Bryant after the game and said, "I thought that quarterback was slow! How'd he catch my world-class sprinter?" Bear Bryant looks at that opposing coach and said, "You have to understand. Your man was racing for six points. My man was racing for his life."

Some of us have to be racing for our lives before we're motivated to stretch. What motivates you? What makes you want to be your best for the glory of God? Think about it for a few minutes. For some people, challenge itself is a stimulant. Others are motivated by dissatisfactions with their present situation. Or we can be spurred on by previous success.

One of the things that helps me stretch is a public commitment, a public goal. I have found that when I tell others what I want to do, it really helps me to keep on track. They can hold me accountable by checking my progress. John F. Kennedy loves to tell stories about his grandfather Fitzgerald. When his grandfather was a boy in Ireland, he would walk home from school with a whole group of boys. There were a lot of very jagged, high cobblestone fences. They were kind of difficult to climb, and some of them were 10-12 feet high, so they were a little dangerous to climb. But, being adventurous boys, they always wanted to go over the walls, but were afraid of getting hurt. One day as they were walking home from school, Fitzgerald took his cap off and threw it over the wall. The moment he threw it over the wall, he knew he had to climb over to get it back, because he didn't dare go home without his cap or he would be disciplined. Throwing your cap over the wall commits you to stretch and do something you would not normally do. I encourage you to begin to throw your cap over the wall.

Vulnerable in the Stretch

Most people are vulnerable when they are stretching. When a rubber band is pulled taut, it's much easier to break. A runner who's stretching for the wire is in a precarious position. If you were to push him a little bit you could knock him clear off his course. Every energy, every muscle, every fiber, is aiming toward a goal, leaving the runner vulnerable.

If you're not stretching, you're in a much better position to defend yourself; your muscles are naturally defensive. Though most people begin their lives by stretching, they soon discover that this position leaves them open to attack, so they begin to withdraw. They start to equate stretching with pain. Before long they're not willing to stretch anymore.

Those who continue to stretch will find themselves vulnerable to criticism. Unfortunately, the road to success is paved with critics. They're ready and waiting to point out how imperfectly other people do what they themselves are unable or unwilling to do.

Jonas Salk, who developed the polio vaccine, was attacked continually for his creative, inventive work in the medical field. He found that criticism came in three stages. The first stage is when people tell you that you're wrong—it won't work. After they've seen you get some success under your belt, they say that what you're doing isn't really that important. Finally, after they see that it's important, they'll say that they knew you would do it all along. If you're stretching, the best defense to these critics is the fruit of your labor. Don't feel that you have to pull out of that stretch position to defend yourself. Just go out and produce the fruit. Those who recognize fruit will appreciate it and those who don't recognize fruit will criticize you whether you produce it or not.

We're also vulnerable to misunderstanding. Often people whose own motives are wrong will feel threatened by us if we are stretching to be our best. They react by questioning the validity of our motives, accusing us of doing our best for some impure purpose.

Not only are we vulnerable to the reactions of others, but we can be vulnerable to ourselves. We are often harder on ourselves than other people are. If we have no goals, we won't recognize failure, but if we're stretching for success, we will fail from time to time. We need to learn how to deal with that. Don't ever let failure become final. Be aware that discouragement is failure's partner. The best way to pull yourself out of discouragement is to surround yourself by people who are encouragers. Get a friend who really understands the value of affirmation, who really believes in you. Do you know the best way to get encouragers around you? Become an encourager yourself.

We've talked about criticism, misunderstanding, failure, and discouragement. Take about five minutes and evaluate yourself: where are you vulnerable?

The Need for Affirmation

The most important time to affirm people is when they are stretching. If you want to be a cheerleader to a friend, be a cheerleader when he or she is really moving out and stretching. Too many people affirm too late. I think there are times when we're afraid to encourage risk takers, because in doing so we identify with them; we join them out there on the limb. If they fail, we fail too. But remember that even a tombstone will say good things about a fellow after he's dead. Don't be a tombstone encourager. Affirm early.

Affirm often. Don't wait for the race to be won, but encourage each step forward. Affirm immediately. The effect of an encouraging word loses its strength as time lapses. If you sense that a friend is starting to slip, give immediate affirmation before the slip has a chance to become a full-scale slide. Affirm personally, and don't be afraid to affirm in front of others. Nothing is more encouraging than to receive honest praise in front of your peers.

Stretching Never Stops

Most people never learn that stretching never stops.
We have a pattern of stretching and resting, stretching
and resting. I understand the need for recuperation and
restoration, but the problem is that most people stretch
a little and rest a lot. Pretty soon they have a vacation
mentality, a retirement mind-set.

Too many people stop learning because they have come
to believe that you go through twelve years of school
and then you go to college for four years and then your
education is over. But a good education really does
nothing more than prepare you to stretch and learn for
the rest of your life. Then there are people who stop trying because of bad past experiences. They say, "I tried
that once before," or "I've already done that." They
allow one failure to put a lid on their abilities.

When you stop stretching, you become *boring*. Nothing
bores me like people who haven't had a new thought in
the last year. They bore the socks off of me. That's why I
think it's so important that in every area of our lives we
continue to stretch.

The other day my father, who is retired and living in
Florida, called me and said, "Son, I just want to tell you
that life is so exciting. I've got more work than I've ever
had in my life. I'm scheduling more meetings; I'm traveling more. My correspondence is getting so heavy that
I've got to get a secretary. Life is not boring at all; I've
been so busy." My dad is in his early sixties now, and I
have no doubt that in his early eighties he'll still be
excited about life. He is determined to live until he dies.

Why do people stop stretching? Let me give you four
quick reasons. The first is that they have surrounded

themselves with people who are both bored and boring. Stay around people who are vitally alive if you want your own blood to continue to flow. This is the reason so many elderly people die fast when they enter retirement centers where there is nothing for them to do. When all of a sudden they realize all there is to do in life is watch the sun set, they're in trouble. They're going to be setting themselves.

Number two, work ceases to be a challenge. For many people, work is nothing more than an assembly line, and so it becomes automatic. That's why we always need new goals, new visions, or new dreams.

Many people stop stretching because they have learned to get by with shortcuts. Nothing is more damaging to growth than getting by with second best. There is a difference between taking shortcuts and working smart. We all want to work smart. Working smart takes less effort but is more effective. Shortcuts not only require less effort, but they're less effective. So I'm not talking about working smart, knowing priorities, and understanding how to arrange your work so you can do it more quickly. I'm talking about settling for less than the best.

I find that many pastors learn early in their careers that they can just open their Bibles, study a text a little bit, and get up and "wing it." They stop taking the time to write their messages out and make sure they have developed some depth. I know many pastors who have to move to a new church every three years because they've used up their resources; they've taken shortcuts all their lives and forgotten how to study.

Many times we stop stretching because we see our value based on our relationships, not our resources. Marriage is one example. If we stretched as hard after our marriages to make our mates happy as we did before our marriages, we wouldn't have marriage problems. After the wedding, we figure that our spouses will love us just because we're married. So we stop stretching, and our marriages stop growing.

Let me apply it in another area—work. I've known people to start a new job and work really hard for six months. Then they become friends with the boss and start slacking off. They mistakenly think a relationship means they don't have to pull as hard on their resources. They stop stretching.

Stretching—Your Finest Hour

Most people will look back at their stretching experiences as their finest experiences. Why? Growth is happiness. The happiest people in the world are growing people.

We have in our society a lot of false hopes for happiness. We have what I call *destination disease*. People think that when they arrive at a certain point, they'll be happy. When they retire, when they get rid of this job, when they take that trip, when they meet that goal—then they'll be happy. They're goal-oriented, and there's nothing wrong with being goal-oriented, but they have not learned to enjoy the journey as much as the arrival. Your happiest moments happen along the way, not at the end of the trip.

There's another false hope for happiness that I call *someone sickness*. That's when you say, "If I could just meet that person; if I could just marry that woman, I'd be happy." But you are the only one who can make yourself happy. No one can bring happiness to someone who is miserable. When we begin to take responsibility for our own personal happiness and realize that it's through growth and growing experiences, even though they may be painful, that we become happy, then we're really going to achieve.

Another false hope for happiness is what I call *backslider's blues*. That's the affliction of people who are always talking about the good old days. They're always talking about the past, which was always better than the present. They see only the good things, neither remembering, nor wanting to remember, the bad times. As the saying goes, "If ifs and buts were candies and nuts, we'd all have a Merry Christmas."

One last false hope for happiness is the problem-free plague. There are many people who want to get in a problem-free society, and they're plagued with that hope. They say, "Boy, if I just wouldn't have problems, I would be happy." No, no, no! Problems have nothing to do with your happiness. In fact, in your stretching periods you will probably have more problems than at any other time, and those will be the greatest times of your life.

Stretching Inspires

Few people stretch all their lives, but those few people inspire the rest of us. There is something within us that is thrilled to see a man or a woman attempt the heroic. The pioneer, the successful entrepreneur, and the victorious athlete all speak to us about the ability of the human spirit to achieve monumental accomplishments when properly motivated. Vicariously we share in their achievements and find hope in our own lives through them. What we need to do is to become inspirers of others, and the only way we're ever going to do that is to throw our caps over the wall. When others see us climbing our fences, they too will begin to climb theirs.

In the earlier part of this century, Charles Lindbergh thrilled the world by flying across the Atlantic. In his story, he tells how as he was going across the United States and over Canada and Newfoundland, he would look down, spotting places where he could land in case of problems. But there came a time when all he saw was the Atlantic Ocean when he looked down. "It was at that moment I realized there was not turning back; there was no place to land." Charles Lindbergh had thrown his cap over the wall, and he inspires us because of it. He stretched.

Put It to Work

Let's get to the application of this lesson. How can we stretch to success? *Discover your potential.* Get near somebody who believes in you. Discovery always comes in an encouraging environment. Find someone who will help you discover who you are and what you can do. Do something that you enjoy. I feel so sorry for people who work in jobs they don't enjoy and live in places they don't like. If you don't like where you live and you don't like your work, why don't you quit your work and move somewhere else? Discover your potential by doing something you enjoy. Then remove the "if onlys" from your life. As long as you have "if onlys"—if only I could be there and if only I could do this, if only I could be that, you'll never discover your real potential, because you'll always be excusing yourself for what you are.

Dedicate your potential. Give your motives to God. If He has your motives, He has everything. Dedicate your potential by giving your best to others.

Develop your potential. You can develop your potential by beginning to accept personal responsibility. Then, realize that God is interested in your development. God is even more interested in your development than He is in your mistakes. Forget your mistakes; start developing. Never limit your potential. Don't you dare sell yourself short. Fifty years ago Johnny Weismuller was the greatest swimmer of all time. Had 50 swimming records. Today 13-year-old girls break his records every time there's a swim meet. Don't limit your potential.

Chapter *Four*

VICTORIOUS BECAUSE
OF A VISION

Helen Keller was asked one time what would be worse than being born blind. She quickly replied, "To have sight and no vision." I've found that if you ask successful people what has really helped them get where they are in life, invariably they'll talk about a goal, a dream, a mission, a purpose—something that has been motivating them throughout the years to become what they have finally become.

Tragically, our world is full of what I would call mundane men, people who see only what is immediate. They only reach out for things they can tangibly put their hands on. They go for the convenient. They never look beyond themselves, and they never look at what they could be. A mundane man may be a truck driver, a bank president, or a schoolteacher. Mundane men can be found in every profession. A mundane man is really someone who lacks depth because he lacks vision. The poorest person in the world is not the person who doesn't have a nickel. The poorest person in the world is the one who doesn't have a vision. If you don't have a dream—a goal and a purpose in life—you're never going to become what you could become.

There is a distinguishable difference between successful and unsuccessful people: successful people are motivated by a dream beyond them. They have a dream that is bigger than themselves; they have something that constantly keeps them going. It's out of their reach, and yet they believe that if they work hard enough, they will someday hold that dream in their hands. That's a successful person. Unsuccessful people are only motivated by today. They are not tomorrow thinkers. They're not looking beyond themselves. They grab with gusto the present, not even taking into consideration what tomorrow may present them.

Dream Stages

When you receive a vision that could change your life or you're grabbed by a dream that could really help you become what you want to be, there's a natural sequence that happens. First there's the "*I thought it*" stage. That's when a dream just flashes by. *Could it be? Maybe this is for me. What would happen if I did that?* That's the "thought it" stage. Every person goes through this stage. Probably not a week goes by in which we don't dream. *Could this be me? What would happen if I did this?* We go from the "*I thought it*" stage to the "*I caught it*" stage. After we think about some of the dreams that we have and the visions that God gives us, we get excited, and we begin to talk about that dream and see ourselves in it.

I think everyone goes through these first two stages. But stage three makes the difference between the person who will be successful and the person who won't be successful. It's what I call the "*I thought it*" stage. After we catch that dream, there's a time when we have to put a deposit down on it. There comes a time when we have to make an investment in it to make it happen. No dream comes true automatically. We have to buy that dream.

The successful person goes into that third stage and buys the dream. They decide to pay the price. But just as the successful person buys it, the unsuccessful person fights it. It's at that stage they begin to rationalize; they begin to think about why it wouldn't work, why it's not possible, and they begin to fight the dream that God may have given them to reach their potential. People who are not going to reach their dreams stop at this third stage. They don't buy into it; they fight it—and they never become what they could become for God.

The fourth stage is the "*I sought it*" stage. This is where desire comes in: we begin to want it so much that it possesses every part of us. Finally comes the "*I got it*" stage: I can touch it with my hands. This is where I say, "It's mine; I'm glad I paid the price; I'm glad I dreamed the dream."

I was in college when Robert Kennedy was assassinated, and I remember one of my college friends coming in and sharing with me that morning that Kennedy had been killed. In the days immediately following his death, there was much written about him in the newspapers. I cut out a quotation of his that I've never forgotten. I'm not sure it was original with Kennedy, but it was said about him, and I hope it can said about all of us. "Some people look at things as they are and say, why? Some people look at things as they could be and say, why not?" There are people who see only what is and constantly butt their heads up against the wall and back away with Excedrin headaches. They haven't figured out that if they stand on their tiptoes and peek over that wall, they will see that there is life beyond. They're always asking, Why did this happen to me? Why am I a victim of my circumstances? But there are other people who have learned to look beyond limitations and barriers. They can see beyond and say, Why not? Why can't this happen to me?

When Hubert Humphrey died, I began reading a lot about his life. He wrote a letter to his wife in 1935, during his first visit to Washington, D.C. Here's what he said. "I can see how someday if you and I just apply ourselves and make up our minds to work for bigger things, we can someday live in Washington and probably be in government, politics, or service. Oh gosh, I hope my dream comes true. I'm gonna try anyhow.

Stopped by a Vision

Let's look at the Apostle Paul. I think one of the key ingredients in his life was his vision. Not only did he see what he was, but he also saw what the grace of God could enable him to become. It was that vision that kept him steady throughout his ministry. In Acts 26:19, when he stood before King Agrippa, he said, "Consequently, King Agrippa, I did not prove disobedient to the heavenly vision." In spite of all the problems he had run into in his ministry, in spite of what was about to happen to him, he had been obedient to the dream God had given him. The vision Paul was given by God did several things for him. First, it stopped him. If we have a great dream, if we have a challenging vision, it will stop us right in our tracks.

> While thus engaged as I was journeying to Damascus with the authority and commission of the chief priests, at midday, O King, I saw on the way a light from heaven, brighter than the sun, shining all around me and those who were journeying with me. And when we had all fallen to the ground, I heard a voice saying to me in the Hebrew dialect, "Saul, Saul, why are you persecuting Me? It is hard for you to kick against the

goads." And I said, "Who art Thou, Lord?" And the Lord said, "I am Jesus whom you are persecuting." (Acts 26:12-15)

Our visions may not be quite that profound. Few of us have a Damascus road experience. But like Paul, if we have a great vision, it will stop us in our tracks and let us glimpse what we have the potential to become.

What happened in Paul's life can happen in our lives. When we see ourselves properly, there are a couple of things that will happen. One, we'll see our position. We'll see who we are. We'll see what we are doing. We'll see where we are going. This can be discouraging because we may think, I'm not accomplishing what I want to accomplish; I'm not being what I want to become. But all people who have the potential for greatness first of all have to see themselves as they are, and usually that's discouraging. When Paul saw that he had been persecuting Christians, when he saw that he had been thwarting the plan of God, when he saw that he had been buying into the wrong religion, no doubt he was discouraged. Remember when Isaiah had a vision of God? It stopped him. He began to see himself, and his first comment was, "Woe is me." In effect he was saying, "Wow! I'm in trouble. I'm not what I should be; I'm not what God wants me to become" (Isa. 6:5).

When we have a vision from God and it stops us, we not only see our position, but thankfully, we also see our potential. We see our possibilities. The good news is that God believes in you, and He will not allow you to see yourself and your problems without allowing you to see your potential. He's not going to frustrate us; He's going to encourage us and help us see what we can become. Isaiah went from "Woe is me" to "Here I am, Lord. Send me" (Isa. 6:8).

Five things happened to Isaiah. He was God, and when he saw God, he saw a holy God. That took him aback. When we see holiness of God, we see our own uncleanliness. Second, he saw himself, and he was that just as God was holy and perfect, he was needy and imperfect. Then he saw others; he looked at the multitudes around him. He saw God, he saw himself, he saw others, and then he allowed God to change him. At that point one of the seraphim picked up the coal from the altar and placed it on Isaiah's tongue. God took him through a purification process. Fifth, Isaiah began to stretch. He began to say, "OK, God, allow me to be a part of this dream. Allow me to reach out and be what You want me to become."

The value of a vision is that it encourages you to give up at any moment all that you are in order to receive all that you can become. In other words, once you've had a glimpse of what God can make of you, you'll never be satisfied with what you now are. You will be willing to let go of whatever might keep you from actually realizing that vision. You can probably think of times in your life when this happened to you. Do you remember when you first fell in love with the person you married? All of a sudden other members of the opposite sex were not that interesting to you anymore. You were willing to trade in the pool for the one.

I have found that you do one of two things in life. You either pay the price now and enjoy later, or you enjoy now and pay the price later. But you will always pay the price. I'm constantly amazed at the short-sightedness of people who are not willing to pay the price now. Some people are short-sighted about their bodies. They're not willing to give up those pleasurable things that are destroying their bodies now in order to gain a few good years later. Some people are short-sighted about their finances. They can't give up any of today's luxuries in exchange for tomorrow's financial security. And some people are short-sighted spiritually.

They are so caught up in the pleasures of today that they can't see the pain of tomorrow: they're not willing to totally sell out for God. They're trying to avoid the price, but the price will always be there. You can either pay it today and enjoy life tomorrow, or you can enjoy life today and pay the price, plus interest, tomorrow. You cannot avoid the price.

I have always been very goal conscious. For that reason, even though Margaret and I had been dating since high school, I decided we would not get married until I graduated from college. While I waited through four years of college, I watched a number of my friends marry during their sophomore and junior years. You can guess what happened to many of them: grades fell, financial hard times hit, and discouragement set it. Even so, they were encouraging me to go ahead and get married. But I remember thinking, You guys weren't willing to pay the price. I'll set my goals and pay my dues.

The time will come when I'll be enjoying a fantastic marriage, plus the fruit of my ministry, and you guys will still be struggling. I can point to five or six of my closest friends from college who are still struggling. They sold their birthright for a mess of pottage. We either enjoy life now and pay for it later or we pay for life now and enjoy the fruits of it later.

Sent by a Vision

When Paul had a vision, it stopped him, but it also sent him. Any God-given dream will never just stop you; it will always send you. The vision or the dream God has for you will allow you to touch other lives. So, Paul was stopped, he saw himself, he saw his potential, and then he was sent. After the vision had stopped Paul, the Lord said to him, in effect, "OK, Paul, you've looked at yourself long enough; stand on your feet."

> For this purpose I have appeared to you, to appoint you a minister and a witness not only to the things which you have seen, but also to the things in which I will appear to you; delivering you from the Jewish people and from the Gentiles, to whom I am sending you, to open their eyes so that they may turn from darkness to light and from the dominion of Satan to God, in order that they may receive forgiveness of sins and an inheritance among those who have been sanctified by faith in me. (Acts 26:16–18

Like Isaiah's vision, Paul's vision would help him touch others. A vision first requires that we see ourselves and then that we see others. No person is successful in fulfilling God's dream for his life until he has begun to positively affect the lives of those around him.

This is the "I bought it" stage. You may have thought it and caught it, but have you bought it? Have you made the decision? That decision requires that you involve yourself in people's lives.

I remember reading an article in 1972 in *Life* magazine. It was entitled, "One Man's Life of No Regrets." It was about a 47-year-old man who had set out at the age of 15 with 127 specific goals in his life. By the time he was 47, he had reached 105 of his goals. He talked about how he had the rest of his life to reach out and grab the other 22. His goals stopped him, and then they sent him. They changed not only his life but the lives of others around him.

Strengthened by a Vision

If the vision is God-given it will stop us, it will send us, and it will strengthen us. As Paul stood before King Agrippa, he talked about some of the setbacks that he had had (Acts 26:19-23). The key is where he says that he has obtained help from God. The goal strengthened him. We receive a visitation from God, and then we pursue our visions for God. He visits us, and as He comes upon us and empowers us and strengthens us, then we begin to fulfill His vision. In 2 Corinthians 11:23-28, Paul writes of many labors and many imprisonments, of being "beaten times without number, often in danger of death."

> Five times I received from the Jews thirty-nine lashes. Three times I was beaten with rods, once I was stoned, three times I was shipwrecked, a night and a day I have spent in the deep. I have been on frequent journeys, in dangers from rivers, dangers from robbers, dangers from my countrymen, dangers from Gentiles, dangers in the city, dangers in the wilderness, dangers on the sea, dangers among false brethren; I have been in labor and hardship, through many sleepless nights, in hunger and thirst, often without food, in cold and exposure. Apart from such external things, there is the daily pressure upon me of concern for all the churches.

Now, what helped Paul to come through all those difficulties? It's very simple. He had a vision. The vision makes the difference. Any problem is a problem when there is no purpose. But no problem is a problem when there is a purpose. How true that is!

When you really have a dream, you aren't a problem-conscious person. When you see a problem, you also see a dream, and the dream that takes you through the problem.

Stretched by a Vision

Paul's vision stretched him; it helped him become what he would never have become what he would never have become without it. The same holds true for us. We will never reach our potential unless we follow our dreams, unless we fulfill our visions.

When I was in fourth grade, I went to my first high school basketball game. I stood in the balcony, looking down on the basketball court and the guys getting ready to play. They were in their warmups, and I'll never forget the moment all the lights went out and the spotlight came on, aimed at the middle of the floor. A drum roll preceded the booming announcement of each player's name. The player would then run out under the spotlight to the sound of thunderous applause. Totally entranced, I turned to brother, Larry, and said, "There's gonna be a day when they'll do that for me!" After the game I went home and formally announced my intention to become a basketball player.

I became consumed with being a basketball player. My dad made a cement drive, put up a backboard and rim, got me a Spaulding basketball, and I began to play basketball in fourth grade. When I got to fifth grade, I played in the little basketball league.

Sometimes we went to that same high school gym to play intramurals. The first time I walked down on the main floor of that gymnasium, looking all around as only a fifth-grader can, I begin to replay my vision. I saw myself in the starting line-up. I sat down where I'd seen those big high school basketball players sit, and I closed my eyes so I could turn the lights off in the gym and hear the drum roll in my mind; then I ran out in the middle of the floor and just stood there like the other guys had. All the other kids watched me, wondering what in the world was wrong with me. I was simply replaying my dream.

I will never forget the night in my sophomore year when the coach said, "You're going to start this evening," and the lights went off. That dream stretched me. During good weather and bad, I was always playing basketball; I was always seeing myself as I could become. That's what a vision will do for you.

There's a difference between a dreamer and a person who has a dream. There are thousands and thousands of dreamers, but there are very few people who have dreams—and there's a world of difference between them. Dreamers talk much but do little. They may hatch up wild plans and ideas, but you never see them happening. Dreamers lack discipline. On the other hand, a person who has a dream talks little but does much. You may not hear all about the dream, but if you watch, you'll see it happen. This kind of person is driven by the dream.

Satisfaction Guaranteed

Let's look at the fifth thing that happened to Paul. His vision, or his dream, satisfied him. When he stood before King Agrippa, it was with a sense of satisfaction that he said, "I did not prove disobedient to the heavenly vision" (Acts 26:19). He sensed great satisfaction in having been obedient, in having followed through on his dream.

One of the mountains of the Alps that is popular with climbers has a rest house about halfway up. Now, for amateurs, it's a good day's climb from the base to the top. if they start out early in the morning, they get to the rest house about lunchtime. The owner of the house has noticed over the years that an interesting phenomenon happens on a regular basis. When the climbers get into the house, where they feel the warmth of the fire and smell the good food cooking, several will always give in to temptation. They'll say to their companions, "You know, I think I'll just wait here while you go on the top. When you come back down, I'll join you and we'll go to the base together."

A glaze of satisfaction comes over them as they sit by the fire or play the piano and sing mountain-climbing songs. Meanwhile, the rest of the group get on their gear and trek on to the top. For the next couple of hours, there's a spirit of happiness around the fireside; they're having a good time in the cozy little lodge. But by about 3:30, it starts to get quiet. They begin taking turns at the window, looking at the top of the mountain. They're silent as they watch their friends reach the goal. The atmosphere in the house has changed from fun to funeral as they realize they settled for second best. Those who paid the price reached the goal.

What happened? The temporary comfort of the shelter caused them to lose sight of their purpose. It can happen to any of us. Don't we all have little sheltered places in our lives where we can retreat from the climb—and lose sight of our goals?

Who are the happiest people in the world? Are they young people? Are they healthy people? Are they wealthy people? No, not necessarily. The happiest people in the world are those who are living out their dreams. In giving themselves to something bigger than they are, they're giving themselves the impetus to rise above their problems. If you want to know real happiness, dream a dream that is bigger than you are; find something you can lose your life in. Jesus said if you keep your life you will lose it, and if you lose your life you will keep it (Luke 9:24). Isn't there something better than watching "As the World Turns" every afternoon?

Isn't there something better than waiting for a vacation every year? Isn't there something better than waiting for retirement by just killing time? Isn't there something better than just settling for average? Average doesn't look so good when you realize it's the worst of the best and the best of the worst.

When I counsel people, I find that their number-one problem is that they've lost their dreams. They've lost their goals; they've lost their purpose. When you lose a dream or your purpose in your marriage, you lose your marriage. When you lose your purpose in your job, you lose your job. When you lose your purpose for your health, you die.

Think of the great men and women who continued to pursue their dreams into old age. Think of people life Moses, who at 80 years of age led 3 1/2 million people out of captivity. Or Caleb, who at 85 years of age said, "Give me that mountain." Or Colonel Sanders, who at 70 years of age discovered "finger lickin' good" chicken. Or Ray Kroc, who after 70 introduced a Big Mac to the world. Then there's Casey Stengel, who at 75 became the manager of the Yankees baseball team. And there's Picasso, still painting at 88, and George Washington Carver, who at 81 became head of the Agriculture Department. There's Thomas Edison, who at 85 invented the mimeograph machine, and John Wesley, who was still traveling on horseback and preaching at age 88.

Don't ever be content with having reached a goal; don't rest on your laurels. History is filled with examples of people who, though they had accomplished great things, lost sight of their vision. When Alexander the Great had a vision, he conquered countries; when he lost it, he couldn't conquer a liquor bottle. When David had a vision, he conquered Goliath; and when he lost his vision, he couldn't conquer his own lust. When Samson had a vision, he won many battles; when he lost his vision, he couldn't win a battle with Delilah. When Solomon had a vision, he was the wisest man in the world; when he lost the dream God had given him, he couldn't control his own evil passion for foreign women. When Saul had a vision, he could conquer kings; when he lost his vision, he couldn't conquer his own jealousy. When Noah had a vision, he could build an ark and help keep the human race on track; when he lost his vision, he got drunk. When Elijah had a vision, he could pray down fire from heaven and chop off the heads of false prophets; when he lost the dream, he ran from Jezebel. It's the dream that keeps us young; it's the vision that keeps us going.

When I went to Arizona for a convention a couple of years ago, the fellow who was in charge of the convention picked me up at the airport. The conference was going to be at the church where he was the pastor. We got in the car, and we hadn't left the airport parking lot before he started saying things like, "I'm really not sure why you're here. I don't know if you've spoken to older people before, but I have heard you before, and you're enthusiastic. The people that are going to be here are going to be mostly retired, and they've worked hard all their lives in churches back East. They've come here to settle down and just enjoy their sunset years." As he talked, I was getting the message that he wanted me to go easy on them, maybe just give the old folks a devotional. His attitude was going against my grain. This guy doesn't understand people, I thought to myself. People want a cause—they need a goal. If you're not yet dead, you must be still alive; you want something to live for, whether you're 18 or 81.

So, on our way to the conference that night, I got my pen out and began reworking my whole sermon. The more I listened to this pastor, the more convinced I became that I had to preach what he didn't want his people to hear. By the time the service had begun, I had developed what I would consider a real motivational message for these old-timers. I got up and shot both barrels of enthusiasm out into that congregation. I preached on the subject, "Why Retire When You Can Reenlist?" I talked about their potential, the experience they had, their wisdom, and the trials they had come through. At the end, I said, "If you'd like to reenlist in your local church and help fulfill a dream and a cause, come forward." The place was packed that night, and about three quarters of those retirees came up to say, "Yes, sir, we want to have a cause." The pastor was wondering what had happened to his saints. It was not his saints that were the problem. They wanted a dream; they wanted a cause. The pastor was the problem. He had lost that dream; he had lost that vision and settled down for second best.

Do you remember the sequence of a successful dream? Let's go through it one more time, because in this sequence there's one more point that I want to give you. The first page is "I thought it," followed by "I caught it," "I bought it," "I sought it," and "I got it." But there is still one more step if you're going to be a great leader. You should move on to step number six, which is, "I taught it." You should never live out a dream without sharing it with someone else. That's discipleship. In the Winter 1983 issue of *Leadership* magazine, Terry Muck writes,

> According to a survey of *Leadership* readers, communicating vision is one of the most frustrating parts of leading a local church. "It is also a task young pastors feel poorly equipped to handle. In a comprehensive 1982 study, one major seminary found that its alumni felt least prepared in their ability to get people working together toward a common goal. Apparently, putting a vision in a form that inspires and energizes is a major hurdle." One fact is true. Leaders who effectively

communicate goals to their followers are paid far
beyond those who do not.

The key is not only getting to the "got it" stage, where
you have the dream personally, but it's passing that
dream on to others.

The Daily Dozen

• *Examine* your life at the moment. The first step toward
making your dream come true is to find out where you are
right now. That takes close scrutiny.

• *Exchange* all of your little options for one big dream.
Every dream has its price.

• *Expose* yourself to successful people. It is true that birds of
a feather flock together.

• *Express* your belief in your dream. Write it down or talk
about it frequently.

• *Expect* opposition to your dream. Every nitpicker who
doesn't have a dream will oppose yours. Regretfully, there
are ten nitpickers for every person with a dream. You will
never rid yourself of them. As long as your understand
that, you won't let them hinder you. Remember that
those who have no dream cannot see yours, so to them it
is impossible. You can't have what you can't see.

• *Exercise* all of your effort, all of your energy, toward the dream. It's worth it. Pay that price?

• *Extract* every positive principle that you can from life. Constantly be on the lookout for anything that will enhance that dream.

• *Exclude* negative thinkers as close friends. You're going to have some friends who are negative thinkers, and no doubt some are members of your family. But if their negative thinking drags you down, which it will, you don't need to spend much time with them. There are people in my family and in my wife's family who are spirit-dampeners. We have chosen, for the sake of our kids as well as ourselves, not to spend a lot of time with them. You may need to put some distance between yourself and your negative-thinking friends.

• *Exceed* normal expectations to make your dream come true. If you're to reach your dream, you'll have to do that which is beyond the normal. Dreams are not achieved by average energy.

• *Exhibit* an attitude that is confident. I believe that if you are outwardly confident, you will become more confident

inwardly. The way we act outwardly affects what we are inwardly.

• *Explore* every possible avenue to reach your dream. Don't let any detour or dead-end street stop you on your way to a dream God has given you. There are more routes up a mountain than just the east side. Go around to the south side. See what else you can do.

• *Extend* a helping hand to someone who had a similar dream, and both of you will climb together. Mountain climbing is not an individual sport. It's a team sport. One holds the line for the other. As we hold the lines for others, we can all make it to the top, and our dreams can come true.

Chapter Five

THE BIGGER THEY ARE, THE HARDER THEY FALL

I want to bring some principles out of the story of David and Goliath that will help us to charge the giants in our lives in a more effective way. Before you read any farther, stop and think for a minute: What is your biggest problem? What giant is standing in your path?

This chapter is dedicated to enabling you to be victorious over some seemingly insurmountable barrier or difficulty in your life. Victory requires more than positive thinking; positive thinking is nothing more than a thought pattern. It requires more than enthusiasm; enthusiasm is only a feeling. It even requires more than action. Victory comes about when we think right about our problems, feel right about our problems, and then act right about our problems. We need more than just a positive mental attitude.

Thinking Right

I read an interesting article recently about Karl Wallenda, the great tightrope artist. He died a few years ago in Puerto Rico, after a 75-foot fall from a tightrope. On one occasion he said, "Being on a tightrope is living. Everything else is waiting." He lived for the thrill of the moment. Wallenda's wife, who was also an aerialist, had some interesting observations concerning what happened before that fateful fall. She said, "All Karl thought about for three straight months prior to walking across the tightrope was falling. It was the first time he'd ever thought about that. And it seemed to me that he put all of his energies into not falling, rather than walking the tightrope." Mrs. Wallenda added that her husband went so far as to personally supervise the installation of the tightrope, making absolutely certain that the guy wires were secure. He had always trusted his crew to do this in the past.

He walked the tightrope with the fear of falling in his mind, and his thinking created his feeling of insecurity; we know what happened. He poured all his energy into not falling, and that's exactly what happened to him. I think that's what often happens to us when we face giants. We look at the Goliaths in our lives in the same way the army of Israel looked at them, and our thoughts focus on not being defeated. That was all they could think about—not being killed, not being destroyed. When we focus on the pitfalls rather than the prize, we often fall right in. We should never allow ourselves to lose sight of our goal, for we may never see it again.

Stone Number One—Check Your Cause

How did David kill Goliath? With a slingshot and a stone. We need some stones to ward off the giants in our lives too. Stone number one—check your cause. That is the first thing I would encourage you to do. Identify your purpose. What is the cause that makes you need to tackle your problems? Is it worthy enough to consume your energy, effort, time, commitment? Is it worth the risk you'll be taking? You can be sure that David had a cause. When he arrived on the scene, the first thing he found was a very frightened Israelite army. The second thing he saw was Goliath—and he realized why they were scared to death. David had a giant of a problem to deal with.

I've found that little minds have wishes, and great minds have causes. Many of us are life Woody Allen, who said, "No matter what I'm working on, I'd like to be doing something else." I know a lot of people like that! They have never developed a purpose great enough to hold them steady or a commitment strong enough to make a real difference. Behind every great accomplishment is a purpose, not a wish. Our purpose is what keeps us from giving up. Behind every enjoyable experience is a purpose, because purpose puts the seasoning in life, and makes it tasty and exciting.

Here's an acrostic that may help you understand and remember what a sense of purpose will do for you, how it will lift you out of the realm of the ordinary. A purpose will cause you to

Pray more than the ordinary person.

Unite more than the ordinary person.

Risk more than the ordinary person.

Plan more than the ordinary person.

Observe more than the ordinary person.

Sacrifice more than the ordinary person.

Expect more than the ordinary person.

A purpose will cause you to spend more time in prayer. If your purpose is bigger than you are, you'll need to continually ask God for His wisdom and strength. Prayer is how the power of God is unleashed. We need to look at prayer as taking hold of God's eagerness, not overcoming God's reluctance. Throughout the Scriptures we are challenged to boldly claim victory through prayer: "Call to Me, and I will answer you, and I will tell you great and mighty things, which you do not know" (Jer. 33:3). "And whatever you ask in My name, that will I do, that the Father may be glorified in the Son. If you ask Me anything in My name, I will do it" (John 14:13-14). "Therefore I say to you, all things for which you pray and ask, believe that you have received them, and they shall be granted you" (Mark 11:24). Through prayer we have the power and privilege to be used of God for a great purpose. The disciples of the first century knew how to pray and claim in faith the power of our omnipotent God to help change the course of history. We serve the same God today.

A purpose will cause you to unite—to look for others with similar goals. A good example of this is found in Genesis at the time of the building of the Tower of Babel. Because the people were united in a purpose, they were able to do things that had never been done before—extraordinary things.

A purpose challenges us to *risk* more. We're willing to put ourselves out a little farther on the limb; we're willing to get closer to our Goliaths.

If we have a purpose, we will do extraordinary *planning* to see it accomplished. If a cause is bigger than we are, it will require our best organizational skills. Goals aren't met by accident.

A purpose also makes us extraordinarily observant. It makes us more sensitive to people and needs around us. We will look for opportunities to move forward.

Having a purpose enables us to sacrifice beyond the call of duty. We're willing to lay more on the line. And last, having a purpose allows us to expect more than we ordinarily would.

What I'm really saying is this: purpose makes the difference between the ordinary and the extraordinary. A person with a purpose does things out of the ordinary, above average. Personality doesn't make a person extraordinary. Neither does intelligence nor education. What makes a person extraordinary is purpose—the consuming desire to accomplish something in life.

There was only one reason for David to charge Goliath: he had a purpose. The God of Israel was being ridiculed by the Philistines because the Israelites were afraid to tackle their problem. Was their God not able to help them? When we're confronted by the Goliaths in our lives, what is it that makes us want to attack? Our first step should be to identify and examine our causes.

Not long ago I picked up an article about a doctor who had studied the care of the elderly. He found that people who lived to be over 100 years of age all had one thing in common. Now, I expected to read about healthful diets and disciplined exercise programs—subjects that make me uncomfortable. But that wasn't it; the one thing these centenarians had in common was purpose. They each had a positive outlook on life. The future looked bright; they had a reason to live.

The Second Stone—Count the Cost

After we check our cause, we need to pick up the second stone with which to fight a Goliath: count the cost. What's it going to cost me to tackle this problem? When God measures a man He puts the measuring tape around his heart, not his head. David not only knew what he wanted, which was Goliath, but he knew what he had to do to achieve his goals; he knew what it was going to cost him.

To defeat Goliath, David had to pay a twofold price. Number one, he had to pay the price of criticism. When he charged his giant, he was going to be criticized.

> Now Eliab his oldest brother heard when [David] spoke to the men; and Eliab's anger burned against David and he said, "Why have you come down? And with whom have you left those few sheep in the wilderness? I know your insolence and the wickedness of your heart, for you have come down in order to see the battle." (1 Sam. 17:28)

Notice that the criticism leveled at David came from his brother. While his enemies laughed at him, his friends and relatives criticized him. They said things like, "You don't belong here. You're too young. You're too inexperienced. You're proud."

I've found that before any great accomplishment is achieved in reality, it's believed in the heart. If we need to hear the applause of the crowd before our Goliath is down, we will never slay him. We have to begin our attack in the face of criticism, believing that the applause will come later.

In addition to criticism, you should count on some loneliness too. I want you to notice that when David charged up the hill, he didn't charge up there with an army. They were all in their tents with their knees knocking. I can picture them, hundreds of heads peeking out their tents flaps, probably ready to run in the opposite direction when David was destroyed. And I can see David, steadfast in purpose, moving up the hill alone. When you face your Goliaths, you won't be backed up by an army either. You will have to face them by yourself.

When I think of loneliness, I think of an Olympic competitor. He displays his personal skill, while the world just watches. No one jumps out of the stands to run with him. I think of Christopher Columbus when he wanted to sail due west to Asia, believing that the world was round. "Oh, no," everyone else said, "the world is flat." I think of Henry Ford and the car. One of my great-great-uncles was a good friend of Henry Ford's. He once told Mr. Ford, "I have no doubt that you can invent an automobile, but once you've invented it, where will you drive it? There are no roads! There will be no place for you to go." My uncle didn't realize that if you have a great enough idea, people will literally move mountains to make that idea become reality. But you have to have the strength of your convictions to launch your dream alone.

Every person who has never killed a giant will tell you that it's impossible. They will tell you it can't happen. So if you set out to confront a Goliath, expect to meet criticism and feel loneliness; it's all part of the process. David understood that. And David Livingstone charted great paths for missions in Africa. One time a missionary society wrote him a letter saying, "We have some people who would like to join you. Do you have some easy access roads to get where you are?" Dr. Livingstone wrote back and said, "If you have men who will come only if there are good roads, I don't want them. I want men who will come even if there is no road at all." Count your cost. It will cost you something to be victorious in battle. You cannot knock giants off easily.

Stone Number Three—Chart Your Course

The third stone that you need in order to knock off your giants is this one: chart your course. Let's look at how David charted his course in 1 Samuel 17:31-40. "When the words which David spoke were heard, they told them to Saul and he sent for him" (v. 31). I think this verse holds a great lesson for us. The moment that you commit yourself to any great project, you will be tested. As soon as David said he was going to charge Goliath, someone was willing to take him up on it.

I think every person who sets a great goal knows the trauma of first publicly declaring that goal. Many times when I knew that God was calling me to do something that was different or difficult, I had to go through an inward emotional struggle to get myself to say it publicly, because I knew that once I said it publicly, somebody would hold me accountable for what I had said. When I was called to preach, I struggled until I was 17 years old to publicly say it, because I knew that once I announced it, my friends and my family would take it seriously. In 1973, as a young preacher, I felt that I should lead to the Lord 200 people who were outside of my church. I remember driving from Chattanooga, Tennessee to Lancaster, Ohio, wrestling with God for the entire eight-hour trip over whether I should declare this goal publicly. I knew that as soon as I told people, they would really jump on it. I declared it publicly, and for a week I knocked on doors and did everything you're supposed to do to win somebody to the Lord Jesus Christ, but nobody was getting saved. On Saturday night when I came in to do some last-minute study in the church office, a friend was out in the lobby, and he said, "Pastor, I've been praying for you all week since you declared you want to win 200 people to the Lord. I just wondered, how many have you won this week?" And I remember telling him, "None—but I'm going to win somebody before tomorrow night." I turned around and walked out of the church. I went clear across town to do some serious soul-winning—and led a couple to the Lord. They were in church the next morning. What happened? The moment you publicly announce that you're going to charge a Goliath, somebody in the crowd will hold you to it. As soon as David said, "I'm going to charge Goliath," what did the people do? They took him to King Saul. David said to Saul, "Let no man's heart fail on account of him; your servant will go and fight with this Philistine" (v. 32). In verse 33, Saul says to David, "You are not able to go against this Philistine to fight with him; for you are but a youth while he has been a warrior from his youth." The moment you commit yourself to a great project, not only will your statements be tested, but others will express their doubts. As soon as you say what you're going to do, there will be the King Sauls of life who will tell you that it has never been done before and you can't do it either.

> But David said to Saul, "Your servant was tending his father's sheep. When a lion or a bear came and took a lamb from the flock, I went out after him and attacked him and rescued it from his mouth; and when he rose up against me, I seized him by his beard and struck him and killed him. Your servant has killed both the lion

and the bear, and this uncircumcised Philistine
will be like one of them, since he has taunted the
armies of the living God." And David said, "The
Lord who delivered me from the paw of the bear,
He will deliver me from the hand of the
Philistine." And Saul said to David, "Go, and
may the Lord be with you." Then Saul clothed
David with his garments and put a bronze hel-
met on his head, and he clothed him with armor.
And David girded his sword over his armor and
tried to walk, for he had not tested them. So
David said to Saul, "I cannot go with these, for I
have not tested them." And David took them
off. (1 Sam. 17:34-39)

When you make a commitment to charge a Goliath, the
third thing that will happen is this: people will want to tell
you how to do it. Can you relate to that? You see, they'll
express their doubts, but when they find they can't talk you
out of the project, then they'll want to give you instruc-
tions on how to handle it. They'll try to put their armor on
you. Saul, who himself was unwilling to face Goliath, was
more than willing to tell David how to do it. Do you know
people like that? The very guy who could not handle the
problem himself was willing to tell someone else how to
handle it.

As a leader, I will listen to anybody. There's no one who
can't teach me something. But the only ones I'm really
going to take seriously are those who have an investment in
my cause and are willing to charge the hill with me. When
they give me their advice, they're putting their lives on the
line with me. There are all kinds of people who are willing
to stay in the background and tell you how to do it—but
they're not willing to take part in it themselves.

Notice that David, when he charted his course, was confident in mapping out his strategy because of his past success-

es. David knew that the God who helped him with the bear and the God who helped him with the lion is the same God who would help him with the giant. God had delivered him before; God would deliver him again. I can't emphasize enough the importance of getting success under our belts. We've got to have some victories. It is winning that gives us confidence. I find that people who won't handle problems are people who have histories of failure; they're afraid of problems.

When I was a kid, I was very frail and anemic. I ate liver all the time—in fact, I ate it so much that I learned to like it—and I had to take medicine to spinach myself up a little bit. Even so I always had a competitor's heart, and I loved to wrestle my older brother, who was much bigger than I. We'd shove all the living room furniture up against the wall, much to Mother's disapproval, and go at it! Dad not only allowed this regular evening activity, he was our referee. Have you ever watched fake wrestling on TV? That's what we did every night—only it was real—and guess who got killed every night for a whole week? So one time Dad said to my brother, "Larry, this week you can't wrestle Johnny. You referee; I'm going to wrestle him." Every night my dad and I would wrestle for 15 or 20 minutes, and I would finally whip him. I would finally get him down and make him say uncle. I felt so good! After I had defeated my dad every night for a whole week, Dad said, "OK, Larry, you and John wrestle again." And my brother never pinned me again. Did I get strong in a week? No, physically I was about the same, but mentally I had grown a lot. All of the sudden I had deduced that if I could beat my father, I could beat my brother. Dad said it took almost an hour the first night. Larry would almost pin me, but I'd think, "Hey, wait a minute! I whipped Dad; I can whip him."

That's what had happened to David. David was mentally tough. So he charted his course based on his past successes.

That doesn't mean we handle our problems the same way every time, but it does mean that our attitude is the same.

Let me give you another acrostic, this one a formula for planning ahead when you get ready to tackle the Goliaths in your life.

Predetermine your course of action

Lay out your goals

Adjust your priorities

Notify key personnel

Allow time for acceptance

Head into action

Expect problems

Always point to success

Daily review your plan

The letter *P* stands for *predetermining your course of action*: decide what you want to accomplish. David knew what he wanted to have happen. He wanted to kill Goliath; he wanted to take Goliath for the glory of God.

After you determine a course of action, *lay out your goals*. Ask yourself, How do I want to achieve that? Think of the course of action as your umbrella; that's your main purpose. Then set goals that will enable you to accomplish your purpose. David decided to take off the armor of Saul, pick up a slingshot he had used before—a proven, trusted victory tool—and take up the stones. Each of these goals had to be reached before his mission was accomplished.

Third, *adjust your priorities*. That's so important! Once you have determined your course of action and laid out your goals, you'll discover priorities you have to discard, because they won't be effective. You'll have to discard Saul's armor, whatever it is, and pick up what you need.

The *N* stands for *notifying key personnel*. David even did that, didn't he? He went to King Saul and said, "Here's what is going to happen; here's what I'm going to do."

The letter *A* stands for *allowing time for acceptance*. After you've predetermined your course of action, laid out your goals, adjusted your personal priorities, and notified the key personnel, you need to allow time for acceptance. Why? Because the world is not used to defeating giants. The more difficult the project, the longer it takes people to accept it. If in your leadership you are finding that some people don't need time to accept some of your goals; it probably because your goals are way too small. You've got to take bigger steps, make bigger plans, meet bigger giants.

Head into action. That comes right after the time for acceptance. Some never defeat their Goliaths because they think that allowing time for acceptance means they have to have a consensus. They think they have to have everybody approve of their plans. You will never kill giants in your life if you need everyone's support. Give them time to understand and accept what you're going to do, but don't expect them to agree with it. They may not vote for it, but allow them time to swallow it, and then head into action.

The letter *E* stands for *expecting problems*. The bigger the project, the bigger the problems. It's always that way. If you're having too easy a time achieving your goal, maybe your goal is not big enough. Don't let problems surprise you; expect them. I once had breakfast with a fellow in the construction business. He made a statement I'll never forget. He said, "I have made my money off everybody else's problems." And he'd made a lot of money! He was willing to tackle what no one else would tackle. What others drew back from and were intimidated by he was willing to take on.

Always point to success. There will always be people pointing in the other direction, aiming you toward failure. But keep your eyes focused on success.

Daily review your plan. Check your position every day. The giants move around on the hillside, and what you did yesterday to kill the giant may not work today.

Stone Number Four—Consider Your Christ

Let's go on the fourth stone we have to pick up if we're going to kill the giants in our lives; consider your Christ. David didn't charge up that hill all by himself. He considered his Christ.

> Then the Philistine came on and approached David, with the shield-bearer in front of him. When the Philistine looked and saw David, he disdained him; for he was but a youth, and ruddy, with a handsome appearance. And the Philistine said to David, "Am I a dog that you should come to me with sticks?" And the Philistine cursed David by his gods. The Philistine also said to David, "Come to me, and I will give your flesh to the birds of the sky and the beasts of the field." (1 Sam. 17:41-44)

That is an example of positive thinking. Goliath said, "Come here, I want to make mincemeat out of you." But there's a difference between positive thinking and positive faith, and in verse 45 we see positive faith.

> Then David said to the Philistine, "You come to me with a sword, a spear, and a javelin, but I come to

you in the name of the Lord of Hosts, the God of the armies of Israel, whom you have taunted. This day the Lord will deliver you up in to my hands, and I will strike you down and remove your head from you. And I will give the dead bodies of the army of the Philistines this day to the birds of the sky and the wild beasts of the earth, that all the earth may know that there is a God in Israel, and that all this assembly may know that the Lord does not deliver by sword or by spear; for the battle is the Lord's and He will give you into our hands." (vv. 45-47)

That's the difference between positive thinking and positive faith. Paul made that great statement, "I can do all things through Him who strengthens me" (Phil. 4:13). This verse includes four positive things. The "I can" is the positive thinking. When Paul goes on to day, "I can do," that's positive action. If your positive thinking is right, it will result in positive action. When he says, "I can do all things," that's positive faith. A less confident person would have said, "I can do some things," but Paul believes he can do all things. He also had positive power. "I can do all things through Him," meaning Christ. When we measure our possibilities, we should do so not by what we see in ourselves, but by what we see of God in us. Our God "is able to do exceeding abundantly beyond all that we ask or think, according to the power that works within us" (Eph. 3:20). We cannot even imagine what God wants to do in our lives.

Stone Number Five—Charge Your Challenge

If you want to be effective, charge your challenge. Go get it! David seized his chance to get into action.

Then it happened when the Philistine rose and came and drew near to meet David, that David ran quickly toward the battle line to meet the

Philistine. And David put his hand into his bag and took from it a stone and slung it, and struck the Philistine on his forehead. And the stone sank into his forehead, so that he fell on his face to the ground. Thus David prevailed over the Philistine with a sling and a stone, and he struck the Philistine and killed him; but there was not sword in David's hand. Then David ran and stood over the Philistine and took his sword and drew it out of its sheath and killed him, and cut off his head with it. When the Philistines saw that their champion was dead, they fled. And the men of Israel and Judah arose and shouted and pursued the Philistines. (1 Sam. 17:48-52a)

I consider that last verse to be the key to the whole story. The reason we need to kill the giants in our lives is this: those whom we lead will never kill the giants in their lives until we first kill the giants in our lives. When did the people shout? When did they charge? They did it after David had killed the giant. When leaders fail to conquer their own problems, their followers never become victorious. This is the number-one problem in leadership in the country. There are too many people in leadership positions who are not successful because they're not facing problems head-on. If they are unwilling to confront their giants, if they are not overcomers, neither will their followers be. When the leader fails, the people fail. When the leader fears, the people fear.

All over the country I see congregations trying to survive in the midst of major problems because they don't know how to deal with them. They don't know how to knock off a giant because they've never seen their pastors do it. Think of how we would release our people if we become giant killers. Imagine what that would do to their faith? The number-one problem in the church is that we're not seeing miracles; we're not seeing God do His work. We think of miracles as history, and we think of victory as history. We ought to pray that God will give us a seemingly insurmountable barrier so that our people can see the power of God at work in us to defeat our giants.

My first church was in a rural area of Indiana. We decided we wanted to have 300 people in our Sunday School. One sincere member of that congregation, Mike, was convinced it couldn't be done. One Sunday he stood up right in the morning service and said, "Pastor, we can't do that." Mike had a sincere heart, a loving, wonderful pure gold heart, but he didn't have an expanded mind. I remember looking at him and smiling, and saying, "Mike, if we do it, will you stand up and apologize and tell this congregation you'll never think small again?" It was kind of a brash thing for a twenty-four-year-old kid to say, but it didn't offend Mike; he said he would. The day we had 301 in Sunday School, Mike stood up, tears streaming down his face, and he told the whole congregation, "I'll never think small again."

I did something for Mike that day. It was great to have 301 in Sunday School; but for Mike it was greater to have the lid taken off his thinking. One of his giants had been slain.

In 1954 there were medical articles that said that the human body can't run a four-minute mile. They said that physically the body was not able to withstand that much pressure. And then what happened? In 1954 Roger Bannister, a young medical student, went out and ran a mile in under four minutes. Today, any miler that's going to have any kind of national recognition runs a mile in less than four minutes. Between 1954 and 1956, 213 men ran under four minutes, all because one guy broke the barrier.

In the 1900 Olympics Irving Baxter high jumped 6'2". People said the impossible barrier was 7 feet—no one would ever jump over 7 feet. Then a guy by the name of

Fosbury figured out that high jumpers were jumping the wrong way over the bar; they shouldn't go over feet first; they should go over head first backward. Everyone else laughed and ridiculed while he worked on an unorthodox way to jump over the high bar. Critics dubbed his method, "the Fosbury flop"—but he "flopped" over 7 feet. Recently an East German jumped 7'8 3/4".

Back in 1956, 15 feet was thought to be the limit for a good pole vault. Then someone discovered that a fiberglass pole gave a little higher lift than the conventional pole. Now a Polish athlete has pole vaulted 18' 11 3/4". Nineteen feet will be the next record, and perhaps sometime down the road, 20 feet. Why? Because somebody broke the record. A giant was killed, so everybody else decided to charge. That's what can happen every day in your life. No matter what your ministry is, the moment you begin to know those giants down, people will say, "We can do that too!" And off they'll go. It gives them permission; it gives them confidence.

What are some lessons we've learned from David's encounter with Goliath?

We fail, not because of big problems, but because of small purposes. Our failures are not caused by giants. Goliaths don't defeat us; small purposes defeat us.

We usually have to charge Goliaths by ourselves. Don't expect a whole crowd of people to gather around you, waving banners and patting you on the back. Whoever steps out first will step out alone.

Small successes lead to greater successes. Begin to have some victories over small things in your life. Make every day a victory over something, and build a track record of success.

Success for most people comes after someone else has done the impossible. Success for the army of Israel came after David defeated the giant. Help someone else be a success—knock off a giant. Remember, the bigger they are, the harder they fall.

What would you say you have learned from David and Goliath? What have you picked up that may help make a difference as you face giants in your life? Take a few minutes to consider what you've learned—then go meet your giants!

Chapter Six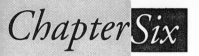

SEE IT, SAY IT, SEIZE IT

There are three levels of living. First is the see-it level, which is the bottom level. Anybody can live on this level. Everybody has the opportunity to see. Now when I say "see-it," I'm not talking about visual acuity; I'm talking about faith's opportunity. Some of us are visually acute; but blind to opportunity.

In my church in Ohio there was a fellow who was a great hunter. We sometimes drove together to Columbus, a 25-mile freeway ride. As we drove, he would say things like, "Did you see that groundhog?" No, I didn't see that groundhog. "Did you see that rabbit?" I didn't see the rabbit. "Did you see that duck?" I didn't see the duck either. We'd drive all the way to Columbus, and he'd see about 10 animals and all I would see was the freeway. All those animals were in my range of vision, but I didn't see them because I had not been trained to look for them. The see-it level of living is faith's opportunity. We can all be looking from the same spot and not see the same thing.

The second level is the say-it level, and that's what I call faith's world. To see it is the opportunity for faith; to say it is the word of faith. That is where we begin to verbally commit ourselves to what has gripped our vision. The Bible is full of say-it faith. The Word of God teaches us, "If you confess with your mouth Jesus as Lord ... you shall be saved" (Rom. 10:9).

Then comes the seize-it level of living. This is the level at which faith becomes action. It's more than verbiage, and it's more than vision—it's a vital action within our hearts and lives.

Since everyone starts on level one, the see-it level, we all have the opportunity to grab hold of faith's opportunity. As you climb the steps, however, fewer and fewer people climb with you. When you get to the seize-it stage, the action stage, you will find yourself in an elite group; most people never climb this high. They have missed faith's opportunity and life's action.

The Example of Caleb

There is an example in the Bible of a person who reached the seize-it level, and his name is Caleb. When we pick up Caleb's story, it is 45 years after he spied out the land of Canaan, bringing back a good report. Now the Israelites are in the process of taking the land for their own. In Joshua 14 Caleb is talking to the elders, those in leadership. "I was forty years old when Moses the servant of the Lord sent me from Kadesh-barnea to spy out the land" (v. 7). That's the see-it stage; he has seen the land. Caleb goes on, "I brought word back to him as it was in my heart" (v. 7). That's the say-it stage.

The vision began to seize him. It not only got into his head through his eyes, but it got into his heart. He began to feel what he had seen. "Give me this hill country about which the Lord spoke on that day, for you heard on that day that Anakim were there, with great fortified cities; perhaps the Lord will be with me, and I shall drive them out" (v. 12). Joshua, having seen

Caleb's commitment to the vision 45 years earlier, gave Caleb the land: Caleb seized what he said he saw. Caleb is not alone in the pages of Scripture. I have found that most great men of God went through these three stages before their visions became realities.

See It—Faith's Opportunity

Moses. Let's look first at the see-it stage in some of the Bible's great leaders. Moses is a prime example of a leader who saw faith's opportunity. When I look at the life of Moses as the author of Hebrews sums it up, I am impressed by the fact that Moses was motivated by his vision.

> By faith Moses, when he had grown up, refused to be called the son of Pharaoh's daughter; choosing rather to endure ill-treatment with the people of God, than to enjoy the passing pleasures of sin; considering the reproach of Christ greater riches than the treasures of Egypt; for he was looking to the reward. By faith he left Egypt, not fearing the wrath of the king; for he endured, as seeing Him who is unseen. (Heb. 11:24-27)

Moses was a great see-it leader, a great visionary. I want you to see four things that Moses' vision helped him to accomplish. Number one, it helped him to make difficult decisions. He refused to be called the son of Pharaoh's daughter. That was a difficult decision; he was giving up his royal position; he was giving up all the pleasures of Egypt. He was able to make that decision because he saw a greater calling, a greater vision.

The second thing that Moses' vision helped him to do was to be willing to pay the price. The price was enduring ill-treatment with the people of God rather than enjoying the passing pleasures of sin. He was going to endure instead of enjoy—because he had a vision.

Third, Moses' vision helped him to live for the eternal and not for the temporal. Because he had a vision, he did not have to live for today; he could live for tomorrow. He considered the reproach of Christ more valuable than the treasures of Egypt. Why? The treasures of Egypt were present, but he was looking to a future reward. He didn't have that reward in his hands as he could have had the pleasures and the treasures of Egypt. Because he was a visionary, he lived for tomorrow instead of for today.

Fourth, Moses' vision helped him overcome fear in his life. By faith, he left Egypt, not fearing the wrath of the king.

I have discovered that having a vision will do the same things for us that it did for Moses. It will help us make difficult decisions. People who cannot make difficult decisions may feel torn between good things. What keeps them from being able to choose the best is that they have no purpose because they have no vision.

A vision will help us pay the price. It provides the motivation for us to give up good things now for better things later. A vision will also help us rise above fear. It keeps us from becoming immobilized by monsters so that we will be able to move mountains.

Caleb. We've already looked briefly at Caleb, but let's see what Caleb's vision helped him accomplish. First, it helped him develop conviction. He says in Joshua 14:7 that when he saw the land, he told Moses that his heart had seized it. His vision gave him conviction. He was able to stand up against the other spies, to follow through on his vision.

His vision helped him obey God. Others' hearts began to melt with fear, but Caleb said, "I followed the Lord my God fully" (Josh. 14:8). Why? Because he had a vision.

It helped him stay young. We all hear about vitamin B and vitamin C, but the best vitamin you can have is vitamin V, the vision vitamin. When people take vitamin V, they are revitalized daily. Age never becomes an issue because they still have a goal, they still have a dream, and they still have a vision. At 85 years of age Caleb was ready to go to war for the land. His strength had not abated. Why? Vitamin V. He had a vision.

His vision helped him secure the land. He eventually possessed it—because he first of all saw it.

I often meet people who are drowning in life's problems. Yet it really isn't their problems that are weighing them down; it's their lack of vision. A big vision will help you overcome any problem, but a small vision or no vision at all will cause the smallest of problems to trip you up and keep you from becoming what you should be.

Abram. The prerequisite for possessing new territory is sight. The story of Abram and Lot provides a great example. When Abram and Lot separated, Abram gave Lot the first choice of land; Lot took the well-watered plains of Jordan. Abram had what was left, which was the supposedly second-rate land. "And the Lord said to Abram, after Lot had separated from him, 'Now lift up your eyes and look from the place where you are, northward and southward and eastward and westward; for all the land which you see, I will give it to you and to your descendants forever'" (Gen. 13:14-15). Abram was encouraged to do three things. First God said, "Look." Then He added, "from the place where you stand." Now, this is more complex than it sounds. He was telling Abram that all the opportunities for being a success could be seen from where he was right then. The roving commentator for the local TV station would have been following Lot down to the well-watered plains of Jordan, because it looked like Lot took the best, but God told Abram to look beyond what looked plush and lush and green and fruitful and to look from where he was standing. He told Abram to see what opportunities lay before him.

Too often we want to go stand on someone else's spot; we want to get on their mountain and look around at their green grass. But God was telling Abram, "Abram, there's no need to run over there where Lot is; you stand right here and look. Where you are standing are opportunities." The good news is that where you are, whatever your lot in life is, under your feet is gold. All you have to do is see it and believe it.

The third thing He told Abram is, "Look in every direction." I don't think it's an accident in the Scriptures that He spelled it out: northward, southward, eastward, and westward. To miss seeing a section was to miss possessing it. He had to spell it out because some of the areas that Abram could see didn't look too promising. Maybe if God had said, "Abram, I want to give you the best land," Abram wouldn't even have looked at some of those areas because he knew the land well.

Vision always comes before victory. James said, "You do not have because you do not ask" (James 4:2). Could it be that we don't have because we don't see? My wife and I know better than to take our son Joel into any store. He's a little Abram.

That little guy can walk into any store and see opportunity. There are very few things for sale for which he couldn't find a use. Be it a toy store or a drapery store, he never fails to find something he desperately needs and thinks he should have. He's always ready to go out and possess the land. We would prefer to possess him and stick him back in the car, because what he doesn't see, he doesn't desire to have. The point is this: to have something you have to first see it.

Focus Your Vision

There are four areas in which we need to fine-tune our vision. First, do I see *myself* correctly? How can we see ourselves accurately? Spend time in prayer and meditation. Notice problems that continually arise in your life. What kind of problems are they and when do they occur? If your problems are similar in nature and they occur in the same types of situations, you've never really dealt with the cause. Ask yourself some questions: What kinds of circumstances cause me to show strong emotion, either positive or negative? What kind of people do I spend my time with? What spiritual gifts do I possess, and am I using them? How am I living in the light of my knowledge of God? If there are areas in which you're falling short, try to identify the reasons why.

The second thing we need to see is our *inner desires*. If you could be anything you wanted to be and do anything you wanted to do, what would you be or do? What would really bring joy to your life? If you can answer this question, you have identified your inner desires. Knowing this will help you reach your potential.

We need to see our resources, both internal and external. What are your personal strengths? What can you draw on to help you possess the land? Do you surround yourself with supportive people? Do you use past experiences to your benefit? Do you take advantage of opportunities as they arise?

Fourth, we need to get a clear sight of our God. We need to see Him as the God "who is able to do exceeding abundantly beyond all that we can ask or think, according to the power that works within us" (Eph. 3:20).

Say It—Faith's Word

In Hebrews 11 there is a list of examples of active faith.
The possessors of this faith are described in verse 13:

> All these died in faith, without receiving the
> promises, but having seen them and having wel-
> comed them from a distance, and having con-
> fessed that they were strangers and exiles on the
> earth.

First, they *saw* the promises—that's see-it faith. Then
they confessed, or said, that they were strangers and
exiles—that's say-it faith.

Steps to Saying It

There are four steps toward possessing a say-it faith. How
do you make your inward belief an outward confession?
First you need the confidence to say what you believe.
Many great dreams die because the dreamers lack the confidence to declare them. Whenever we are unsure of ourselves or our projects, we usually remain silent. We don't
say it because we want to save face.

Saying it takes commitment. Many great dreams die
because dreamers lack the commitment to declare them.
Other people cannot follow our inward hopes; they follow
our visible commitments. It's seeing the dream consume us
and seeing the commitment that makes us act on that
dream that causes others to follow it. Commitment is contagious. People will only catch what has caught you.

The third step to say-it faith is good communication.
Many great dreams die because dreamers lack the communication skills to get it across. This is very important. There
are four ways that people learn: listening, discussing,

watching, and discovering, or participating. Discovering, or participating, is the most effective way to learn. You need to help your people discover that dream for themselves by allowing them to participate. They need to hear about it, discuss it, and see it happening. You will not have effectively communicated your dream, however, until they participate in it.

If we're going to say it, there's a fourth thing we need, and that conviction. Many great dreams die because the dreamers lack conviction to act on them. There's a difference between commitment and conviction. Commitment keeps me going when things get tough. Conviction keeps others going when things get tough. People around us are motivated by emotion, our conviction, that tangible sense of morale. People do not follow a leader because of character; they follow a leader because of conviction. People do not do things because it is right; they do things because they feel that's it's right. When we act on our conviction, others are drawn to us. Without conviction we may communicate truths, but we'll develop no disciples. We will have people who have the right answers, but we won't have people who live the right lives.

Saying it, then, requires confidence, or knowing it; commitment, doing it; communication, showing it; and finally, conviction; feeling it. To have say-it faith you have to know it, do it, show it, and feel it, and then you'll be able to say it.

Seize It—Faith's Action

Few will cross the Jordan to seize the prize. I think there are four reasons why some of us get right to the edge of the river and then don't go on across and possess the land. First, we're too close to success to risk failure. Fear of failure probably keeps more people from positive action than anything else.

The second reason that we do not seize it is that this level requires discipline. If you're going to act on your dream, it takes more than just sitting around on the sofa. You have to roll up your sleeves and go to work. It does not take any discipline to dream, but it does take discipline to make those dreams real.

The third reason that many people do not seize it is that this level divides the concerned from the committed. I have found that you can get almost anybody to agree to almost anything. You can get almost anybody to show some kind of concern for something. But there are few people willing to leave the ranks of the concerned to join the committed.

This level takes time. If you're going to seize your dream, you'll have to make a time commitment. You can say your dream in a moment, but you can seldom seize a worthwhile dream in less than a lifetime.

Secure That Dream!

How are we going to secure the dream of a life? I would suggest six things:

State dreams
Examine motives
Consider options
Utilize resources
Remove nonessentials
Embrace your challenges

The first thing you do is state your dreams. Write them out on a piece of paper. Look at them. Then examine all your motives. You have to ask yourself, *Why am I doing this? Do I have pure, right motives?* If the motive isn't right, the dream will die. Make sure in the beginning that your motive is right.

Consider all your options. Now that you have stated your dreams and examined your motives, sit down and consider all of your options. How many ways can you reach this goal? There is more than one option. Everybody needs a backup plan; everybody needs a plan B and a plan C and a plan D. Next, utilize your resources. Find people around you who have a similar dream and work with them.

The letter *R* stands for *removing your nonessentials.* Get the excess baggage off your back, anything that keeps you from achieving your dream. The letter *E* stands for *embracing your challenges.* Picture difficulties in front of you and practice reacting positively instead of negatively. Learn to wring out of those challenges the best that God has for you.

In February 1973 when bus ministries were really big, I went to a conference in Lynchburg, Virginia. Jerry Falwell was talking about buses, and he challenged the 5,000 of us there to get a dream for a bus ministry. God began to speak to my heart, saying, "John, you could you in one year as many people on buses as what your church was averaging when you came." Our average attendance had been 418. I didn't even have a bus. I remember going back to the Holiday Inn and lying on the floor saying, "God, do You really want me to do this?" Falwell had said, "Tomorrow, we're going to give you a card and you're going to write down your name and the number you're going to have on buses within one year. And you're going to bring them forward and we're going to read them." I thought, *Oh, no, they're going to read this in front of 5,000 people from all over the world!* I wrestled with it all night. The next day I took a card and put 418 on that card—and I didn't have a bus! With fear and trembling I handed in my card, and it was read in front of 5,000 people. I thought, *This is the worst thing I've ever done in my life.* But I became motivated because I had said it. Falwell wrote a letter to my church board telling them my goal, and I had to go out and raise money for buses before we ever brought it to the board. The great thing is that in one year's time, literally one year from that day, we had 438 people on buses. Why? Because we went out and seized it.

A First Step Toward Seizing Your Dream

What do you see God challenging you to do or be in the next year? Whom will you share this dream with in the next two weeks? How will you seize this goal and make it become a reality? Take fifteen minutes right now and write down the answers to these questions on a 3" x 5" card. Then write down some steps of action you're going to take to seize that dream. Place your card in a visible location. Read it in the morning, act on it during they day, evaluate it in the evening, and pray about it at night. Don't let this opportunity pass you by. There are many people in this world who see it. There are some people in this world who say it. But there are only a few people in this world you seize it. Filling out this card is the first step toward seizing your dream.

Chapter Seven

THE 101 PERCENT PRINCIPLE

The effectiveness of our leadership is determined by our ability to relate to others. Leadership is influence. Whether it's effective, positive leadership or ineffective, negative leadership, when people are leading others, they have influence—what they say, what they think, and what they do influences those who follow them.

Your relationship with others determines how you will influence them. Are they under your care? Are they accountable to you? Are you consistent and approachable? Do you project a positive attitude? Your relationships with the people around you will do more to determine your effectiveness as a leader than anything else. Too often we try to separate leadership from relationships. We look at leadership as position, title, or a name.

Jesus' Relational Leadership

John 10 gives us a biblical understanding of relational leadership. Jesus, describing the Good Shepherd, says,

> The sheep hear his voice, and he calls his own sheep by name, and leads them out ... He goes before them, and the sheep follow him because they know his voice. And

a stranger they simply will not follow, but will flee from him, because they do no know the voice of stranger. (John 10:3-5)

There are three components of relational leadership in this Scripture passage. The first is that the shepherd knows his sheep intimately. His relationship with them is such that he recognizes them instantly. The sheep know his voice, and he knows their names. He is personally acquainted with each one.

The second component of relational leadership is that the relationship is built on trust. The shepherd not only knows the names of his sheep, but his sheep trust him. They hear his voice and come to him, but they will run from a stranger. From this we can learn that leaders must be worthy of their followers' trust.

The third component is that relationships are modeled. The shepherd walks ahead of his sheep, and they follow him.

Someone asked chief executives of major companies in the United States to name the characteristic they wanted most in potential employees. By far the great majority of these executives said that they wanted to see more than anything else in people who came into their companies was the ability to work with other people. Of course they want them to have certain abilities and skills, but more than that, they want people who can work well with others. If you can relate well with others, you can go survive almost any situation in life. John Rockefeller, the builder of giant corporations, said, "I will pay more for the ability to deal with people than any other ability under the sun."

A survey was sent out to 2,000 employers, asking respondents to check the files of the last three persons they dismissed from their jobs and tell why they were fired. In two out of three cases, the answer was the same; the employees could not get along with other people. People did not lose their jobs because they lacked skills; they lost their jobs because they lacked ability to relate effectively with others.

We're going to deal with two things in this chapter; handling conflicts in relationships, which I find to be the number-one problem of people in leadership positions, and creating effective relationships.

Handling Conflicts

The secret to handling conflicts successfully is to live according to the 101 percent principle. If there is someone under your umbrella of leadership who tends to be obstinate, find the 1 percent on which the two of you agree, and give it all you've got—100 percent of your effort and ability. Let that 1 percent shred of agreement be the tie that binds you together.

There's a tendency for us to generalize and idealize relationships. Remember the Parable of the Lost Sheep? One sheep disobeyed and disappeared; it left the security of the flock to go out and do its own thing. The shepherd could have said, "We're better off without you—be some lion's dinner!" But no, the shepherd left the 99 that were secure and went in search of the 1 that was lost (Luke 15:4-6). That's a perfect example of the 101 percent principle. The shepherd looked until he found it; he expended a great deal of energy to develop that relationship with the very one who had not been in kilter with the rest of the gang. That's the 101 percent principle.

And I want to give you ten commandments for handling conflicts.

I think they'll be helpful to you because all of us have times when we have to take a relationship that's not healthy and try to bring healing to it.

Ten Conflict Commandments

Follow the 101 percent principle. I had a friend in my last church who had caused all kinds of difficulties. He had done the same with the two previous pastors. In fact, I'm pretty sure he was the reason both of them left the church. For months I thought and prayed about ways to develop a relationship with him. I was looking for that 1 percent. He had his wife had adopted two children into their family, and we had adopted two in our. One Halloween night I took my daughter, Elizabeth, who was then about two years of age, to his house and knocked on the door. I'd already programmed her to go over and give him a big hug and tell him she loved him. She did and he melted. As he stood there crying, I knew I had found the crack in his tough exterior and the 1 percent that we had in common—adopted children. That began to build a relationship that became very successful. That's the 101 percent principle.

Love people more than opinions. Anyone who loves his opinions more than he does his friends will defend his opinions and destroy his friends. People who are not effective in relationships usually have a higher regard for their opinions than they do for people. We need to step back and look at what is really important to us. Is it helping or hindering our relationships with people?

Give others the benefit of the doubt. We usually rule ourselves with our hearts, but we rule others with our heads. We have mercy on ourselves but not on the other person. If you want to build relationships, follow this rule: when working with yourself use your head; when working with others, use your heart. Give other people the benefit of the doubt.

Learn to be flexible. Thomas Jefferson once said, "In matters of principle, stand like a rock. In matters of taste, swim with the current." In my last church when they were decorating the sanctuary, I really didn't like what they were doing, but I also realized that it wasn't that important. If the issue is evangelism, I'm not going to waver for anybody—that's a matter of principle. But if we're talking about the color of the carpeting or the stain on the pews, I'll swim with the current. Learn to be flexible in your life. The greater the man, the more flexible he is. Good leaders learn how to say, "I'm sorry" more quickly than followers. Effective leaders know how to back down; they don't constantly feel the need to defend their rights; they've learned to differentiate between principles and taste; they've learned to be flexible.

Provide an escape hatch for the person in conflict. I have watched people defend their actions, not because they knew they were right, but because their pride kept them from backing down. It takes a strong leader to allow someone who has been defeated to ease out of a situation and save face. Once the point has been made, back off.

Check your own attitude. Many times wrong leaderships develop because of wrong attitudes. You need to ask yourself questions to help you know whether your attitude is right or wrong. For instance, if you're having conflicts with several people, there's a good chance the problem is you, not them. Ask yourself, Am I constantly in conflict, or is this an exception? If it's an exception, your attitude is probably fine. The attitude with which we view people determines to a large extent our perception of how they feel about us. Check your attitude.

Don't overreact to conflicts. You're going to have conflicts; don't make them worse by overreacting to them. Don't drop a bomb when a slingshot will work. If you expect conflicts, you will be better prepared to handle them sensibly.

Don't become defensive. You never win in relationships when you're defensive. A secure leader knows how to say, "I'm sorry. I was wrong. I misunderstood. Please forgive me." The moment that you defend yourself, the moment that you stand up for your rights, you're going to start a battle. We never resolve differences by being defensive.

Welcome the conflict. Make it a learning experience. Most of us will never enjoy the conflicts, but we can be thankful for them if we learn from them. Conflicts will either give you ulcers or understanding: you choose which it will be.

Take a risk. Many people do not handle conflict in relationships because they are afraid to put their hands out first. If my relationship with you is shaky and you extend your hand toward me in a gesture of friendship, how do you feel if I don't clasp it? First, you feel ridiculous standing there with your hand in the air. Then you feel rejected. Many people don't handle their conflicts because they don't want to be rejected. They're unwilling to take that risk.

When I realized that I was going to be a leader, I sat down one day and wrote down all the ways a leader can be hurt. After I wrote them down, dozens of them, I categorized them. I decided that leaders will always be hurt. Don't let anybody sell you on the idea that everybody's going to love you all the time. If you are out front leading people, you will be hurt. The issue is not will you or won't you but in what way will you be hurt? I decided that I would be hurt because I trust people and make myself vulnerable to them. I know people who say, "I won't get close to people, so they won't hurt me." I've watched people build themselves into glass cases; they make good mannequins but poor leaders. Because I am willing to be hurt in that area, I find that there are people I have trusted, people I have believed in, who have grown because I risked getting close to them; I risked being rejected by them. Many times more often than not, it's worth the risk. Allow yourself to be vulnerable.

Cultivating Good Relationships

Fortunately, we don't always have to handle conflicts. We do have some good relationships. How can we make them better? In John 10 we can find three things to do to cultivate relationships: know them, grow them, and show them.

Relationships start with knowing, continue with growing, and climax with showing. Know them: Jesus called His sheep by name. Grow them: they heard His voice and came to Him. Show them: Jesus walked ahead of His sheep, and the followed Him.

Know them. Let me give you the ABCs of beginning effective relationships. Acknowledge your need for others. For your relationship to be cultivated effectively, you have to admit that you need other people in your life. Paul teaches that "there are many members, but one body. And the eye cannot say to the hand, 'I have no need of you'; or again the head to the feet, 'I have no need of you'" (I Cor. 12:20-21). A complete Christian is filled with God's Spirit but it also complemented by different gifted friends. Friends are essential. Acknowledge your need of them. Until you do that, you'll never cultivate effective relationships.

Believe in the value of others. Carlisle said, "A great man shows his greatness by the way he treats the little man." The value you place on people determines whether you are a motivator or a manipulator of men. Motivation is moving together for mutual advantage. It's all of us moving together because it benefits all of us; manipulation is moving together for my advantage. There's a difference. With the motivator, everybody wins. With the manipulator, only the "leader" wins.

Concentrate on people, not programs. The only things that God will ever rescue from this planet are His people. Therefore, if you want a ministry of permanence, you must build into the lives of others. Changing programs won't establish permanence; changing people will. Some of the most miserable people I know are program changers and builders. On the other hand, the happiest people I know are people builders and changers. Where are you going to put your life? Concentrate on people.

Grow them. If you want to help people grow, you need to be available to them when they need you. People going through hard times have deeply felt needs that you can reach out to meet. As you do, you will find your relationship with them deepening. Timing is more important than time in a relationship. Walking into the lives of people when they really need you is more important than being with them all the times when they don't really need you. Timing is essential.

Be a reliable leader. Relationships grow on consistency; they shrink on moodiness. Be approachable: have you ever wanted to see somebody who had tremendous mood swings but hesitated because you didn't know whether that person would love you or bite your head off? As a leader, be reliable so your people can always feel comfortable coming to you.

Be a reassuring leader. Relationships grow in an atmosphere of affirmation. Most people are insecure; because they need encouragement, you need to be an encourager. Margaret and I recently had a talk with our daughter's gymnastics instructor. He has had trouble grasping the importance of affirming people: he's quick to tell the kids in the class when they do something wrong, but he doesn't know how to say, "That was good. You're doing well there." We encouraged him to use some positive reinforcement with Elizabeth. Affirm your people. That's how they grow.

Be a resourceful leader. Relationships grow when someone has answers to questions. Become a problem solver. Have something to contribute. We all like to be around people who can stretch us, teach us, and help us grow.

Show them. People do what they see. In cultivating relationships we have to model for others good people skills. People do not care how much you know, but they know how much you care, and they know how much you care by the way you act, not by what you say.

In studies of the leadership of American businesses, it has been shown that executives spend three-fourths of their working days with *people.* The largest single cost in most businesses is *people.* The most valuable asset of any company is its people. All executive plans are carried out, or fail to be carried out, by people. Our relationships with people will determine the success of our leadership. We can either work with people or war against them. We can be plows or bulldozers: the plow turns over the earth, stirring it up, cultivating it, making it a good place for seed to grow; the bulldozer scrapes the earth, pushing obstacles aside. Both plows and bulldozers are useful instruments, but one wrecks while the other cultivates. The plow type of leader sees in people riches waiting to be uncovered and cultivated; the bulldozer type of leader sees in people obstacles to be destroyed. Be a cultivator!

Chapter Eight

SOLVE OUR PROBLEMS, BUT SAVE OUR PIGS

When I conduct church leader's clinics, I ask the pastors to tell me all the ways they can think of to grow a church. We take about 15 or 20 minutes, and I fill up a blackboard with ways to get a church growing. We have on that board every essential ingredient for building a church. After reviewing the list, I point out to them that we all know how to build a church. We already have 50 church growth books on our shelves. We already have all those answers. The issue is not whether we know how to build a church; it's whether we're willing to pay the price to make it happen.

One time when Jesus went over to the Gadarene country, a couple of demon-possessed men met Him. He cast the demons out of them and sent the demons into a herd of pigs. The pigs rushed into the sea and drowned (Matt. 8:28-34). Until Jesus came, there had been a real problem in that community. Every time people went near the graveyard, the demon-possessed men came out, wild and naked, and attacked them. But the people weren't happy when their pigs drowned, even though the demons were disposed of too. They wanted to get rid of the demon-possessed men, but they didn't want to lose their pigs.

They remind me of people who want God to solve their problems without it costing them anything. They want all the solutions, but they want them for nothing.

There are some observations about this incident that begin to float to the surface. The people themselves were unwilling to pay the price to see the problem solved. I think that's the most obvious lesson. They wanted to get rid of the demon-possessed men, but they also wanted to save their pigs. It is also interesting to me that the demons didn't want to leave the Gadarene country. They wanted to stay right there. They obviously knew a good thing when they saw it; they found the people in that area easy prey.

We don't want to be confronted with changes or problems. Even when God Himself brings them into our lives, we want to escape them. We want deliverance without disturbance. We want the benefits without the bills. We want success without sacrifice. But it just doesn't happen that way. We cannot afford to drift into a lifestyle that places repose above results. We must welcome the changes that God's Spirit brings and accept them on His conditions and not ours. And it's up to us to set the pace for those who are following us, whatever the cost.

Let's talk about the costs of leadership. What do we really have to pay in order to have credibility, power, and authority in our leadership?

Leadership Means Discomfort

If you are going to be a successful leader, you are going to experience a great amount of discomfort.

In *Success* magazine in October 1985 there was an excerpt from Doing It Now by Edwin C. Bliss (Scribners) that really grabbed me.

We live in a culture that worships comfort. During this century we have seen the greatest assault on discomfort in the history of the human race. We have learned to control our environment with central heating and air conditioning. We have reduced drudgery with machines and computers. And we have learned to control pain, depression, and stress. We even provide electronic antidotes to boredom with television sets and video games. Most of this is to the good, but unfortunately it has created an impression that the purpose of life is to attain a blissful state of nirvana, a total absence of struggle or strain. The emphasis is on consuming not producing; on short-term hedonism rather than long-term satisfaction. We seek immediate gratification of our desires, with no penalties.

Life just doesn't work that way, at least not for many and not for long. One of Benjamin Franklin's favorite sayings was "There is no gain without pain." The great goal of becoming what one is capable of becoming can be achieved only by those who are willing to pay the price, and the price always involves sacrifice, discomfort, unpleasantness, and even pain.

Our Gratification Culture

What are some of the signs in today's society of the pursuit of immediate gratification? How about fast-food restaurants? Credit cards? Abortion clinics? An abundance of divorce lawyers? The list could go on and on. We want to play; we don't want to have responsibility. We want the position and the paycheck, but we don't want to do the work.

Consider the life of the Apostle Paul, one of the greatest leaders in the first century. He understood perhaps better than any of his peers that we have to pay the price to solve our problems. In 2 Corinthians 11:23-29 Paul describes the price he paid for his apostleship, the cost of his success in leadership. There are three things I want to draw out of this chapter as we look at the relationship between leadership and discomfort.

Paul would tell us to *never get comfortable*. When you look at all the affliction he went through, you can see that Paul never thought that he had a claim on comfort. When he wrote about being beaten, shipwrecked, and abandoned, he wasn't asking for pity. He was simply describing his very real experiences. He understood that if comfort is our highest aim, we will miss out on the riches of the kingdom of God.

An American professor was talking to a Christian from the Soviet Union about Christianity in both lands. The Russian woman commented on the difference between receiving Christ in the United States and receiving Christ in the Soviet Union. In America the new Christian is led to a comfortable church and a padded pew, while in the Soviet Union the new believer is prepared for death. Paul tells us not to get comfortable. A person cannot be committed to comfort and at the same time be committed to Christ.

Never allow for plan B. When I say that, I'm not talking about administration. Wise leaders understand that something may go wrong, and they have to cover their bases with subsidiary plans, but this is not a lesson on administration. This is a lesson on paying the price; there is no plan B in the area of commitment; either you are committed or you're not. Get rid of the exit signs in your life. As long as there is a way out, a fire escape, you'll be tempted to take it rather than pay the price. You don't have to survive. The Apostle Paul didn't have to survive; he was committed beyond the point of survival. He had no plan B to fall back on.

Never fall into a maintenance mind-set. Nowhere do you find that the Apostle Paul was satisfied to just maintain the work. He never settled for the good when the best was a possibility. He pressed on, not leaving it up to his coworkers to carry on the work. What I'm saying here is that Paul did not have a maintenance mind-set; his goal was not just to maintain the status quo. He was willing to make waves and be unpopular at the cost of his comfort. Don't be content to carry on when you need to press on.

Leadership Means Dissatisfaction

Dissatisfaction is a tool God can use to motivate us to greater things. I'm not saying we will be great leaders if we are unhappy. Miserable leaders have a great capacity to make miserable followers. When we lose our drive and motivation, we're in danger of losing our vision.

The average church in America, regardless of denomination, has about seventy regular attenders, because that's about how many people it takes to survive. Generally speaking, a congregation of seventy can afford to buy that acre plot of ground, turn the lights on, and partially pay a pastor. That is the survival level, and once churches get there, many of them stop growing because they can meet their own basic needs. Dissatisfaction doesn't set in unless they look beyond their basic needs and examine their overall purpose.

John Wesley was one who understood that leadership means dissatisfaction. He averaged three sermons a day for 54 years, preaching more than 44,000 times altogether. To do this he traveled by horseback and carriage more than 200,000 miles, or about 5,000 miles a year. He was greatly devoted to pastoral work. During a later period in his life, he was responsible for all the churches in England. To get his work done, he rose at 4 every morning and worked solidly until 10 at night, allowing brief periods for meals. At age 83 he was upset to discover that he could not write more than 15 hours a day without hurting his eyes. At age 86 he was ashamed to admit that he could not preach more than twice a day and he was angry that he would sleep until 5 a.m.

Charles Spurgeon was known as the prince of preachers. Like Wesley, he was not satisfied with just being a great orator; he had a passion for the work of God, and he was never satisfied with the number of souls that he had won. At the age of 30 he preached to 5,000 people at Metropolitan Tabernacle, and he still wasn't satisfied. He was once invited to lecture at a university where all of his expenses, his wife's expenses, and his personal secretary's expenses would be covered, and in addition he would receive $1,000 per lecture over 50-day period. Spurgeon, however, turned down this offer, suggesting that instead of taking their $50,000, he would stay in London and attempt to win 50 souls for Jesus Christ.

I was privileged to meet E. Stanley Jones when I was in high school. My dad set up an appointment with him, and we had 15 minutes together. He signed a couple of books for me and talked about how great it was to be in the ministry. He was woven from the same fabric as these great men were. In the twilight of his life he wrote these words from his beloved India, where he was a missionary: "I have often said, half jokingly, that when I get to heaven I will ask for 24 hours to see my friends and then I shall go up to my Master and say, 'Haven't You a world somewhere which has fallen people who need an evangelist like me? Please send me there, for I know of no heaven beyond preaching the Gospel to people.' That is heaven to me. It has been and it ever shall be."

We have been talking a lot about the Apostle Paul, a man who was not satisfied and was not about to quit as he pressed toward that high mark. But there are other men and women in the Bible who were driven to greatness by dissatisfaction with their present conditions. Nehemiah was fairly well off as the cupbearer for the king in the royal court. He was surrounded by luxury, but he was willing to leave all of that to go back and help rebuild the wall of Jerusalem. Or consider Esther, the queen who chose to risk death in order to rescue her people from suffering. Joshua and Caleb could have settled for the wilderness with all of the other people, but they were unwilling to settle for second best. Why live in the wilderness when you can live in the land that flows with milk and honey? Moses could have stayed in Pharaoh's court and enjoyed all the pleasures and the riches of Egypt, but he chose to lead his people out.

Leadership Means Disruption

You show me a person that is in a strategic leadership position and I'll show you a person who will be disrupted. We must get used to disruptions because working with people means there are no guarantees of smooth sailing. Just about the moment we think we're going to accomplish a lot on our agenda, another hurting, needy person comes along.

We have to be like an airline pilot. We know our destination, but we have no control over the weather. Unexpected squalls may make it necessary for us to vary from the flight plan. I was flying from Phoenix to San Diego recently and the weather was pretty bad, rainy and foggy. We started our descent, and I thought we were going to make it until all of a sudden we were in a big cloud. Up we went, circling again. That pilot understood something about flying. He had a time schedule; he wanted to get there at 9:10 in the morning, but he also understood that bad weather patterns may necessitate changes. Instead of 9:10, it may be 10:10 or 10:20 or it may mean going to an alternate airport and reaching the original destination some other way.

Like the airline pilot, we leaders will often have to deal with disruptions—sometimes very unpleasant disruptions. The issue is whether we *respond* or *react* to those disruptions. To react means to act negatively. To respond means to act positively. If you go to your doctor's office, and he prescribes some medicine for you, your body will either react or respond to that medicine. When you come back three days later, the doctor may tell you that your body is reacting to the medicine—he means that your body isn't allowing the medicine to accomplish its purpose. Or he may say that you're responding to that medicine—he means that the medicine is healing your body; you're getting well.

When we have disruptions, do we react or respond? I need to continually remind myself of the importance of responding. People who are schedule oriented, who have their to-do lists, and who have strong goals will always have some tension over disruptions. We have to remember that leadership is more than taking a pen to our to-do lists and marking off numbers. Leadership is meeting needs. I'm afraid sometimes we're marking off numbers instead of meeting needs, and that keeps us from being as effective as we could be.

One key to being an excellent leader is not to let disruption throw you: handle your disruptions but don't be consumed by them; keep your eyes on the goal. Too many people detour around the need in order to hit the goal, or they meet the need but forget the goal. We have to do both. We must minister to the need as we press on to the goal.

A good example of somebody who knew how to deal with his disruptions positively was the great boxer Gene Tunney, who took the heavyweight title from Jack Dempsey. When Gene Tunney was in World War I, he broke both his hands. His doctor, who was also his manager, told Tunney that he had brittle hands; he would no longer be a boxer. But Tunney decided to try a strategy change. Instead of relying on the hard punch, as he had before, he became a strategic boxer; he learned to move well, to score points, and to be an artful dodger. He changed his strategy but not his goal. That is exactly what we have to do with our disruptions. We have to change our tactics, manipulate our circumstances, but continue to aim for our goal. I have found these three guidelines to be helpful in dealing with disruptions.

Number one: Find out the specific will of God for your life. Nothing will keep us on track better than knowing what God's purpose is for us individually.

Number two: Don't give in to the desires of the flesh. If you give in to the flesh you will always take the easiest way out. Make yourself do what has to be done, and you will develop character. As you exercise your character-building muscles, you'll find they become stronger each time they're used.

Whenever you are going to do something great for God, there are 27,000 people around you that will try to tell you why you can't, shouldn't, and won't. All they are doing is testifying to their own experiences. They haven't paid the price for greatness, so they don't understand how you can do it. Effective leaders, however, leaders who have paid the price, know the value of character-building exercises.

They know that they can not give in to fleshly desires, whether their own desires or the desires of other people.

Number three: Don't try to survive. Look at Galatians 1:15-17. You will see these three principles in action. Once Paul saw his goal, he looked neither to the left nor to the right for the easiest path; he simply headed in the direction in which God's finger was pointing. His goal wasn't to survive—and yours shouldn't be either. It is amazing what will happen in your leadership when you do not gauge the happiness of your life or the greatness of your day by how easy it was.

"Have a Good Day!"

Do the circumstances of your day have to be smooth and easy for you to have a good day? Some people's only happiness comes on vacation—so they can only be happy two weeks out of the year. It's a sad thing when people can't enjoy the problems of life. It's a sad thing when you rise up in the morning and realize that it's going to be a bad day because you're going to work, where there are problems that you don't want to deal with. It's a sad thing when you start looking for an escape instead of a challenge.

We have developed a society in which people would rather take the easy way out; we have become a relief syndrome culture. This type of society does not make good leadership training ground. But those who are willing to pay the price will make it, and the world will sit back and wonder how these successful men and women ever got so lucky. Luck has nothing to do with it; they were simply willing to do what all the rest of the people were unwilling to do.

What conditions do you set on your service to God before you'll be happy in ministry? I would encourage you to put down the book as you finish this chapter and spend some time answering that question. Write down what you need to have before you'll be happy. Is it a place where you must live? Is it a salary you must receive? What conditions must be met?

Are we really attacking the problems in our personal lives? We're not in a Boy Scout camp; we're in the army of God. We need to trust God for the courage to go forth and pay the price to help build the kingdom.

Chapter Nine

YOUR PROBLEM IS NOT YOUR PROBLEM

You can tell it's going to be a rotten day when you call Suicide Prevention, and they put you on hold. You can tell it's going to be a bad day when you turn on the news and they're showing emergency routes out of the state. You can tell it's going to be a rotten day when you car horn goes off accidentally and remains stuck as you follow a group of Hell's Angels on the freeway. Have you ever had a day like that? I think we all have. Yet as I work with and study people, I find that they do not all attack their problems in the same way. In fact, I meet people who have huge problems and yet seem to be just whistling along, making out fine; then I meet others who have relatively small problems and they're devastated by them. I have concluded that your problem really is not your problem. Surface problems do not make or break us.

Let me give you some examples. I've done a lot of marriage counseling, and I've seen couples with incredibly large problems decide that they really want to live together and make their marriages work, and they go out and do it. I've had other couples whose problems appear very small. They're a little bored, but they just need to make a few changes and their marriages could be revitalized.

I've watched their marriages fall apart and end in divorce.

I've watched people who had incredible financial problems work their way out of trouble. I've watched other people with small financial problems sink, unable to handle the stress.

It is popular in our society to believe that we are victims of our situations. Society looks at a person and says, "That poor person was born on the wrong side of the tracks and doesn't have a chance." Society emphasizes the problem rather than the person. That's a major mistake. Your problem is not your problem. If you can get the person right, the problem will be fine.

How We Respond to Problems

In one of our Sunday night baptism services, a fellow walked into the baptistry and shared a testimony the like of which I had never heard. When this guy was fourteen, his sister died. Two years later his father was killed. His first two marriages ended in divorce. His oldest daughter died of cancer at the time of his second divorce. Last year his brother was killed during a robbery at his place of business. Grief piled on top of grief caused this man to renew a bad relationship with drugs and alcohol, which caused his third marriage to fall apart. For a guy in his early thirties, he had known a lot of tragedy. And yet at the end he talked about how God had changed his life and given him a bright outlook. There was a smile on his face, he was confident in God. His focus had shifted from his problems to God's promises. Your problem is not your problem

We respond to problems based on two things. We respond to problems based on what we see and what we seek. What we see is determined by our perspective in life and our level of discernment. What we seek is our desires, our values, and our purpose. Before we can understand and tackle problems effectively, we must identify what we see and what we seek. If I can see the problem but lack the desire to solve it, I'll begin to observe problems as they are, but I'll never solve them. To flip that coin, if I desire very much to take care of my problems but don't see them in the right light, I will never be as effective as I could be.

What We See

The Apostle Paul viewed problems accurately. In 2 Corinthians Paul writes about how we are handicapped on all sides.

> We are afflicted in every way, but not crushed; perplexed, but not despairing; persecuted, but not forsaken; struck down, but not destroyed.(2 Cor. 4:8-9)

Paul had been through shipwrecks, beatings, humiliation, and imprisonment, but he saw that the difficulties he was experiencing were very small in comparison with the glory of God (Rom. 8:18). Paul overcame his problems because he saw them in the right light.

So often we take a little speck of a problem and make it a huge barrier in our lives. That's usually because we wee the problem in the wrong light. We don't see it in the light of God's glory.

One day little Bobby's father came into the front room and saw the boy looking out on the street through the big end of a telescope. He said, "Son, that's not the way you look through a telescope. If you look through it that way, you make the objects look much smaller. A telescope is to make things look bigger." But Bobby smiled and said, "Daddy, the bully who's always beating me up is out on the street. I turned the telescope around because he's my main problem, and I want to see him smaller than he really is." Most of us, instead of taking the big end of the telescope and reducing our problems, take the small end of the telescope and magnify our problems so that they look much bigger than they really are.

Past Experiences

We see our problems based on three things, past experiences, present environment, and personal evaluation. Let's start with past experiences. How we have handled problems in the past will greatly influence how we view them today. A sculptor begins his work with a chunk of granite, a mallet, and a chisel. The novice expects a chip of the rock to fall every time he hits the chisel with his mallet, but often nothing happens. After a while he lays down his mallet and chisel, too discouraged to go on. Why? Because every time he strikes the chisel he expects to see a tangible result. The professional working by his side has been doing it for years. He patiently takes that mallet and taps that chisel, and to the inexperienced eye, nothing's happening at all. The veteran knows that a chip doesn't have to fall every time the chisel is struck, because he understands that every time he strikes the chisel, he weakens the stone. If he's patient long enough, the piece he wants to chip off will depart from the main rock.

Seeing your problems based on your experience can be good or bad. If we've had good experiences in handling problems, we will be able to handle them in the future; if we've had bad experiences, then we will probably continue to do so until we get a better understanding of how to deal with difficulties.

A couple went camping in the mountains, and their guide said, "Now, you'll see snakes, but don't worry about it; they're not poisonous." Even though the man a tremendous phobia for snakes, he went hiking alone the next day. When he got back to the cottage where they were staying, his clothes were torn, and he was battered and bleeding. His wife said, "My goodness, what happened?"

He said, "Oh, I was hiking on one of the high trails and I saw a snake. I jumped off a 50-foot cliff."

She said, "But honey, don't you remember, the guide said those snakes weren't poisonous." He said, "They don't have to be poisonous if you jump off a 50-foot cliff." The damage was already done. What was his problem? His problem wasn't snakes; it was fear of snakes. His bad experiences in the past caused him to see the problem wrongly.

Present Environment

We also see our problems in the light of our present environment. Here is a key idea you need to remember: the problems surrounding us are not as crucial as the people surrounding us. We are not overcome by our problems, but if the people around us don't know how to handle problems, then we may be overcome.

There are two ways to respond to an environment filled with problems. We can be like the gardener who took great pride in his lawn. He kept it beautiful. One year his lawn was besieged with dandelions. He tried everything and still couldn't get rid of them. Finally, in his frustration, he wrote the Department of Agriculture explaining all the different dandelion deterrents he had tried and asking what he should do next. The answer came back from the Department of Agriculture, "Try getting used to them." That's not what he wanted to hear. That's not what we want to hear either, but sometimes it's the best advice we'll get. The person who expects to live in a problem-free society is going to be as frustrated as the fellow who thought that he was going to rid his lawn of all the dandelions.

I saw a cartoon the other day which showed a little boy in a car watching his dad outside in the pouring rain fixing a flat time. The boy has the window down, and he's asking his father why this is happening to them. The father looks at the boy and says, "Son, don't you understand? This is life. This is what is happening. We can't switch to another channel."

There's something else that we need to realize. We may always have dandelions in our yards, but we don't have to let those dandelions mess up our lives. During the Second World War a young soldier married a woman and brought her to his post in the California desert. She didn't like the desert; she didn't like the barrenness; her husband was away on active duty most of the time and she was very lovely and bored. Finally she wrote her mother and said, "Mom, I'm coming home. I just don't like the desert, and I don't like the dryness, and I don't like the fact that my husband's gone. It's an ugly place to live." Her mother wrote back to her these two lines: "Two men looked out through prison bars; one saw mud and the other saw stars." That young wife got the message; she decided to look for stars. She began to learn as much as she could about desert flowers and cacti. She studied the language, folklore, and traditions of the Indians who were her neighbors. By the time her husband's tour of duty was over, she had become so engrossed with the desert that she wrote a book on it. Her problem was not her problem. It was how she saw it.

In the fifteenth century in Europe, the whole continent was filled with despair. It was probably the most discouraging time in European history. In 1492, in the *Nuremburg Chronicle*, a German wrote that the end had come; there was nothing left worth living for. At the close of his book he left several blank pages on which he proposed that the reader fill in any discouraging events or situations that he had left out. The next year, 1493, a young buck sailor returned to his Portuguese port with the most exciting story. In the midst of this negative environment, Christopher Columbus came home saying, "Guys, there's a whole new world out there. Get your eyes off your problems. Rip those pages out of your book!" Christopher Columbus was not willing to let the environment of his day determine his dream; he refused to let present problems order his future.

Personal Evaluation

We tackle problems our own size. Big people tackle big problems, and small people tackle small problems. The better a person's self-image, the more willing he or she is to take a risk and handle a big problem. The more fragile a person's self-image, the less willing she or he is to tackle a big problem.

Problems can stop you temporarily, but only you can stop yourself permanently. We cannot continually handle problems in a way that is inconsistent with the way we see ourselves. If you evaluate yourself as a person of worth, then you will begin to tackle big problems. One of the ways you can tell whether you're growing emotionally and spiritually is by the size of the problems that you're willing to tackle.

What We Seek

The size of your problem is determined not only by how you see it but by what you seek in life. Again, your problem is not your problem. Problems defeat us when we lack purpose in life. Goal-oriented people don't let problems deter them from their goals. If they want to reach them badly enough, they're going to reach them.

The night before my son's first soccer game, his coach sat the kids down, and she said, "I'm really not interested in winning this year; I'm interested in having you kids learn how to play soccer—learn the rules, the fundamentals." I understood what she was saying, but I was so proud of my boy, Joel, when he blurted out, "But Mrs. Jones! I want to win!" My last advice to him was to get the ball and go for the goal.

People who regularly allow themselves to get sidetracked by problems are people who have no clear purpose in life. When we have a purpose, when we really seek and desire the best of life, our problems begin to shrink. Here's the way it works. As our purpose increases, our problems decrease. As our goal decreases, our problems increase.

Learning Instead of Leisure

Our problems are no longer problems when we seek learning instead of leisure. You show me a person who loves to learn about life, and I'll show you a person who handles problems well. On the other hand, people who want to live lives of leisure, to whom life is nothing but a big vacation, become frustrated with their problems. M. Scott Peck, a psychiatrist, has written several best-selling books in the last few years, including *The Road Less Traveled*. Peck had decided to do some case studies on the subject of evil. As he did the case studies, he became convinced that evil was a reality, and he became a Christian. In The Road Less Traveled (Simon and Schuster) he writes, "It is in this whole process of meeting and solving problems that life has its meaning" (p. 16). Peck says that life doesn't have meaning unless we learn how to handle our problems. He said, "Problems are the cutting edge that distinguish between success and failure. Problems call forth our courage and our wisdom; indeed, they create our courage and our wisdom. It is only because of problems that we grow mentally and spiritually...It is through the pain of confronting and resolving problems that we learn. As Benjamin Franklin said, 'Those things that hurt, instruct'" (p. 16). Notice what he says about people who want to avoid the pain of problems: "Fearing the pain involved, almost all of us . . . attempt to avoid problems. We procrastinate...forget them, pretend they do not exist. We even take drugs to assist us in ignoring them, so that by deadening ourselves to the pain we can forget the problems that cause the pain" (p. 16). Then he gives the clincher. He says, "This tendency to avoid problems and the emotional suffering inherent in them is the primary basis of all human mental illness" (p. 17).

The writer of Hebrews said of Jesus, "He learned obedience from the things which He suffered" (Heb. 5:8). Problems create situations in which we can grow. The very things we want to avoid in life are the things that nurture us and shape us into the persons we should be. The author of the Book of Hebrews doesn't say that Jesus learned obedience *in spite* of the things He suffered; He said that He learned obedience *from* the things He suffered. Effective leaders have learned this principle, and they almost *welcome* problems into their lives, knowing that it will drive them closer to God and closer to the people with whom they must relate. They have discovered that dealing with problems successfully develops a sense of security, not only in themselves but in Christ Jesus.

Holiness Instead of Happiness

If you study the lives of those who have suffered greatly, such as Helen Keller and Joni Eareckson Tada, you seldom find skeptics among them. The skeptics are the people who have not suffered a great deal themselves, but who have been in the observation towers watching others suffer. They're the ones who ask why. They're the ones who become callused.

Seeking holiness rather than happiness is a hard thing to do in the culture in which we live, because so much is geared to happiness—whatever makes you feel good. In a secular society, happiness is the aim of life. In a spiritual society, holiness is the thing that we strive for. Jesus said, "Blessed are the pure in heart" (Matt. 5:8). That word *blessed* means "happy." Happiness is really found in holiness. But if we try to bypass holiness in our search for happiness, we'll miss it altogether. Happiness is a by-product of holiness; it's a benefit of living a pure life, rightly related to God, self, and others. So if you want to live a happy life, seek to live a holy life.

Solutions Instead of Sympathy

When we seek solutions instead of sympathy, we begin to see our problems in a different light. A woman had been confined to a wheelchair all her life, and a friend who was trying to encourage her said, "You know, afflictions really color life, don't they?" The woman in the wheelchair replied, "Yeah, but I choose the color." A lot of people would have their problems solved if they would just go for the solution, instead of sympathy. We need to realize that our problems are going to be there until we tackle them. Some people choose to hang on to their problems because they enjoy having other people feel sorry for them. I would challenge those people to dare to attack their problems. It's far more gratifying to receive admiration than to receive pity.

I want to close by giving you some problem-solving principles. We handle our problems based on what we see and what we seek. If we see our problems correctly and if we have a goal that is bigger than our problems, there's no problem that we can't solve. The happiest people on earth are not people without problems. The happiest people on earth are people who have learned to appreciate the possibilities for growth that problems bring.

Problem-Solving Principle

Never believe any problem is unsolvable. These six words will give you the right attitude toward problem solving. Whenever I deal with somebody who has a problem, that's the first thing I tell them. Now you may be thinking that there are some unsolvable problems. But I would reply that they're only unsolvable to you. Don't bring everybody else into your arena: speak for yourself. I don't know how to solve every problem, but that doesn't mean every problem is unsolvable. It just means that I haven't found the right person to help me; I haven't worked hard enough on it; I haven't worked long enough; I haven't thought it through. I need to bring in some other resources. Every problem is solvable.

One day in an upper-level doctoral seminar in mathematics a professor wrote an unsolved problem on the blackboard. Mathematicians had been trying for years to solve this problem. The professor was trying to emphasize to the students that there are no easy answers. He told them, "This problem is unsolvable, but I want you to spend the whole hour trying to solve it." One student came in about five minutes after the professor had given the assignment. He sat down, saw the problem on the board, and began working on it—and he solved it—all because he had never heard anybody say it was unsolvable. I wonder how many problems you and I have not solved only because we've heard there's no solution. The first key to handling problems is to get the right mind-set: every problem is solvable.

Define your problem clearly on paper.

You need to see it before you. Don't think your problem; write your problem. Until you can see it, there's a danger of confusing the symptoms with the problem. By writing it down clearly you can separate the symptoms from the real problems. Once you begin to visualize the whole issue, your mind can begin to see solutions.

Organize to divide and conquer your problems.

Generals who understand effective military strategy do not attack all fronts simultaneously; they look for a weak area up at the front and they attack that spot until they break through. This particular tactic works in any kind of warfare. If you have a problem that needs attacking, divide it into parts. Suppose you look at it and see five areas of difficulty; ask yourself which area you could handle most quickly. Then take care of that need. Now the problem has been reduced a little. There are not five parts, just four. So take the next part—and keep going until the problem is gone.

List people and other idea sources that might help you solve your problem.

Begin to collect resources that can help you solve the problem—books, tapes, people. No man is an island, and no man solves problems by himself. This is an area that is too often overlooked in problem solving. People too often try to solve their problems by using their own limited resources instead of using the expertise of outside help.

List all the possible courses of action that you can think of.

Write down five or six possible solutions. Many people are not problem solvers because they only try one solution. If that doesn't work, they decide the problem has no solution. I have found that if I take the time to write down all my options and then begin to attack the problem from different perspectives and from different viewpoints, at least one option will be a workable solution.

Visualize these different courses of action.

Think through the process before you try to actually attack the problem. You may be able to eliminate some of your options, because it will be obvious that they won't work.

Choose the best course of action and get going.

Don't stop at choosing—get going. Don't play the philosopher, who sees the problem but doesn't seek the remedy. Look at the problem, choose the best course of action, and go after it.

Never let problems stop you from making the right decision.

So many times we are tempted to live with problems because if we solve them, someone may get hurt. Don't forfeit the right solution for an easy way out. This is especially crucial in spiritual leadership, because we tend to do that which is most palatable to those we are leading. We don't want to hurt anybody; we don't want to rock the boat. I learned a long time ago that true leaders will make the right decision regardless of it palatability to others.

I've also learned that a lot of people never solve their problems because they wait. Even after they know which option to take, they wait, hoping that the problem will eventually work itself out. Thomas J. Peters and Robert H. Waterman, in their book In Search of Excellence (Harper and Row), make the point that a laboratory may produce solutions, but it doesn't make those solutions work. You can stay in the lab with the mice all day, but your problems won't dissolve. You have to take your solution out and introduce it to the problem.

What you see and what you seek determine your success or failure.

Success in problem solving is more related to the person than the problem. You may not choose your problem, but you do choose your response. It's not what happens to you; it's what happens in you. Your problem is not your problem—once you see it correctly and once you seek high goals in your life.

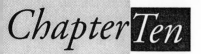

Chapter *Ten*

FAILURE IS NOT FINAL

This may be hard for you to believe, but successful people experience failure almost as often as unsuccessful people. In fact, on the average, successful people fail two out of every five times they attempt something and unsuccessful people fail three our of five times. That's not a lot of difference, is it? Actually, there are several similarities between the person who fails three out of five times and the person who fails two out of five times, even though one would be classified as successful and the other one would be classified as unsuccessful.

The first similarity is that all fail. There's not one person who does not experience failure. The second similarity is that we all fail often. We don't just fail once and walk gingerly through life so that we'll never fail again. Failure is something that we experience every day. And third, we will continue to fail until we die. Death itself is the only thing that's going to keep us from failing. Sometimes I have a feeling that people are trying to tiptoe safely to the grave without goofing up somewhere along the way.

Why is it that failure destroys some and builds up others? How can I allow failure to make me a better person? Too many people concentrate on failure instead of on success. Too few concentrate on success instead of on failure. Herein lies the key.

Have you ever heard a person say, "I'm not going to make a mistake here; I'm going to avoid that pitfall"? Then they do exactly what they were trying so hard to avoid. What happened is that they concentrated on the fall, failure, the fault, the problem that was looming out in front of them. As the proverb goes, as a man "thinks within himself, so he is" (Prov. 23:7).

Ray Meyer, basketball coach for DePaul for 42 years, had 42 consecutive winning seasons before he retired a few years ago. One season his team had a 29-game winning streak at the home court; then they lost a game. Reporters were anxious to get in the locker room to interview Meyer to ask him about that loss and to see how it affected him. He was all smiles; he said, "This is great. For the last ten, twelve days we've been thinking about the winning streak. We've been trying not to lose, every game. Now that we've lost a game, we can go back to concentrating on winning." Those who concentrate on failure program themselves to fail.

One day when the Raiders were in Oakland, a reporter visited their locker room to talk to Ken Stabler. Stabler really wasn't known as an intellectual, but he was a good quarterback. This newspaperman read him some English prose: "I would rather be ashes than dust. I would rather that my spark should burn out in a brilliant blaze than that it should be stifled by dry rot. I would rather be a superb meteor, every atom of me in magnificent glow, than a sleepy, impermanent planet. The proper function of man is to live, not to exist. I shall not waste my days in trying to prolong them. I shall use my time." After reading this to the quarterback, the reported asked, "What does this mean to you?" Stabler immediately replied, "Throw deep." Go after it. Go out to win in life.

Treat Failure as a Friend

**The second observation I want you to see is that too
many people treat their failures as enemies**. They look
at a flop and see a foe. This kind of thinking, in itself, is a
mistake; failure should be treated as a friend. Your reaction
to failure determines what you do with it. If you treat your
failure as a foe, for example, you'll hide it. Whenever you
fail in a certain are, you'll want to get out of that area,
whatever it is—a job, a marriage, a relationship, even a
hobby. If you treat your failure as a foe, you will take your
mistakes too seriously. You'll be ridden with anxiety. Every
mistake will be a life-or-death situation. On the other
hand, if you can see failure as a friend, a helper, then you'll
react positively to it. Only when you're honest and open
about a mistake can you learn from it. When you stop
and think how many times you've really blown it, it seems
a shame to let those failed attempts go to waste. So learn
from your mistakes—and then learn to laugh at our mistakes. No failure is significant enough to sink a person.

When I was pastoring my first church, a college friend was
also serving his first pastorate about 20 miles down the
road from me. We got together once or twice a month for
meals with our wives. Being brand new at the job, I was
making lots of mistakes—blowing it in a big way every
day! So when we came together I would share my flops
and failures. After two or three dinners, I realized that
Mike wasn't communicating; he and his wife were on the
defensive. His wife was saying things like, "Oh, Mike
wouldn't do that," or "Mike has never let that happen."
My wife, on the other hand was saying, "You should have
seen John handle that!" and, "John blew it royally yesterday." Mike never seemed to make a mistake. If there was
ever a problem at his church, it was the people's fault.

I did a series of meetings for him after his first year, and over dinner one night he was talking about the "ding-a-lings" in his church. "That ding-a-ling won't do this, and this ding-a-ling won't do that." After about 30 minutes Mike's conversation was making me nauseated. I thought, *I can't let this go on forever*, and I put down my fork and said, "Mike, I want to tell you. Do you know why you have so many ding-a-lings in your church?" He put down his fork and said, "No, but I'd like to know." So I told him, "It's because you're the biggest ding-a-ling of all." Suddenly, my digestion improved tremendously, but now Mike couldn't eat!

Two years afterward he called me on the phone to say he was going to leave these ding-a-lings and go to another state, to a really *good* church. He hadn't learned a thing from his failures because he saw them as foes. I remember hanging the phone up and telling Margaret, "Mike's going to another church in another state. I give him six months and he'll find ding-a-lings there. If he doesn't start admitting that he's the problem, that he needs to make some changes, he's going to have more problems." Sure enough, he lasted about six months. This time, it was not only the ding-a-lings in his congregation, but it was the ding-a-ling district board, the ding-a-ling district superintendent, and all the other ding-a-lings around him. So he decided to build an independent church. The last time I heard, he was out of the ministry. What happened? He had always looked at his failures as enemies, and he had always blamed them on someone else.

There is truth in the statement that a person is not a failure until he or she places the blame on someone else. Remember Jimmy Durante, the comedian with the big nose? Many people would have taken that nose and hidden in the corner of life—but not Jimmy. Someone asked him one time how he managed to accept his larg-er-than-life nose, and here's what he said, "All of us have schnozzles." He meant that we all have peculiarities. If our "schnozzle" is not on our face, it's somewhere else—maybe in our mind or in our habits. When we admit those schnozzles instead of defending them, regardless of where they are, we can begin to laugh at ourselves, and when we laugh at ourselves, the world will laugh with us.

Take a moment and write down the last big mistake you made. It should take about three seconds to remember it. How did you react to it? Is it your friend? Or is it your foe?

View Failure as a Moment

Too many people, when they fail, erect a monument to their failure and spend the rest of their lives paying homage. Not enough of us view failure as a *moment*—a fleeting experience. Do you make a monument when you fail, or do you look at it as just something that happened in a moment and is over and done with? Charles Kettering said, "Virtually nothing comes out right the first time. Repeated failures are fingerposts on the road to achievement. The only time that you don't fail is the last time you try something and it works. One fails forward." I like the expression, "fails forward." Fail forward toward success.

People make monuments out of their mistakes by saying things like, "I tried it, and it didn't work. They said it couldn't be done, and they were right." Mark Twain said that if a cat sits on a hot stove, the cat will never sit on a hot stove again. The problem is, the cat will never sit on a cold stove either. The cat just won't sit on stoves, because every time he sees a stove he sees a burning fail-ure. Abraham Lincoln wisely stated, "My great concern is not whether you have failed, but whether you are content with your failure."

What else do people put on their monuments to failure besides "I tried it and it didn't work" and "They said it couldn't be done"? How about "I wish I had done that"? There are people who spend their whole lives wishing instead of getting out and doing. They never venture into the arena of action; they sit sadly on the sidelines and wish.

Others say, "I'll never get hurt again." They stay so far away from anything that is risky that life will pass them by. They'll see the joy of the risk takers, but they won't share in it.

Another common inscription on monuments to failure is "I can't change. It's just the way I am." This goes on monuments of people who say, "Leaders are born, not made, and I'm not the leader. I grew up on the wrong side of the tracks. I can't help myself."

There's a curious thing about people who build great monuments to failure: they don't want to accept responsibility for the construction. They're not willing to take blame. They find it much easier to attribute their failures to other people. Their philosophy of life is, "My circumstances make me who I am."

View Failure Inwardly

My fourth observation is this: too many people have too broad a view of failure. They're too quick to judge an attempt as a failure. If they don't see immediate outward positive results, they see a major mistake. Failure is not the external result; it's the internal activity.

Thomas Edison was once experimenting in search of a natural rubber. In his search he had 50,000 failures. His assistant said, "Mr. Edison, we have made 50,000 experiments, and we have no results." He was ready to quit. he viewed failure outwardly. Edison replied, "Results! We have had wonderful results. We now know 50,000 things which won't work." Thomas Edison knew that there was only one thing that was failure, and that was quitting.

So often people who fail frequently follow this philosophy: if at first you don't succeed, destroy all the evidence that you ever tried. They view failure outwardly. What the world judges as obvious failure is many times not failure at all. If you study history, you'll find that the world has put labels of failure on some events that have been some of the greatest successes of mankind. Some examples: the Iowa banker who told Alexander Graham Bell to remove that toy (a Bell telephone) from his office; the Hollywood producer who scrawled *Reject* on the movie screenplay for *Gone With the Wind*; the fellow who was Henry Ford's greatest investor, who in 1906 asked that his stock be sold; Mr. Roebuck, who sold his part of the Sears, Roebuck firm for $25,000 because he thought it would never fly. (The last I read on Sears was that they sell $25,000 worth of goods every 16 seconds.) Do you view failure from the outside or from the inside?

Successfully Fail

Too many people fail, and then they never use that failure to their benefit. There is such a thing as a successful failure. Anytime you have learned from a mistake, you have made a major step toward success.

I read a great article on leadership not long ago in which the author discussed the fact that one characteristic that distinguishes successful leaders and followers is that successful leaders learn from their failures. Let me just quote a couple of statements. "Leaders use their energy well because they learn from failure, and they can therefore reach higher goals. Almost every false step is regarded by them as an opportunity, not as the end of the world. They are convinced that they can learn and, more important, that their organizations can learn from failure."

Tom Watson, Sr., who founded IBM, had a top junior executive who spent $12 million of the company's money on an experiment that failed. The executive put his resignation on Watson's desk, saying, "I'm sure that you want my resignation." Watson said, "No, I don't want your resignation. I've just spent $12 million educating you; it's about time you get to work." Watson knew that there is such a thing as successful failure.

We successfully fail when *it stirs us to keep trying.* The setbacks that look as though they will finish us off can spur us on to come out on top. A Louisiana farmer's favorite mule fell into a well. After studying the situation, the farmer came to the conclusion that he couldn't pull the mule out, so he might as well bury him. He got a truckload of dirt, backed up to the well, and dumped it on top of the mule at the bottom of the well. When the dirt hit the mule, it started snorting and tramping. As it tramped, it began to work itself up on top of the dirt. So the farmer continued to pour dirt in the well until the mule snorted and tramped its way to the top. It then walked away, a dirtier but wiser mule. What was intended to bury it turned out to be its salvation. That's a successful failure.

We successfully fail when *we see our mistakes and are willing to change.* The greatest mistake we make is not correcting the first mistake. When we see where we went wrong, we should make every effort to make sure that it doesn't happen again.

We fail successfully when *we discover our true selves*. In reading the biographies of great men, I've been impressed with two things. One, some of the most successful people in the world started out as failures; two, because they failed, they found themselves and their purpose in life. I'll give you a few examples. Nathaniel Hawthorne was fired from his position in a custom house in Salem, Massachusetts. He came home after losing his job feeling utterly defeated, and his wife said to him, "Now you can write the book that you've wanted to write all your life." Out of that came *The Scarlet Letter*. James Whistler failed at West Point. Then he decided to try painting. We all know his success. Phillips Brooks started out as a teacher, but he couldn't make it in the classroom, so he went to seminary and eventually became an outstanding preacher. These men were successful failures.

Never Quit Because of Failure

Too many people never start because of failure; too few never quit because of failure. Samuel Johnson said, "Nothing will be attempted if all possible obstacles must first be removed." Have you ever not started something because you wanted all the conditions to be perfect before you began? If this is your criterion for taking a risk, you'll never accomplish anything. Perfect does not guarantee success; if anything, its a hindrance.

Starting is the first step to succeeding. Too many of us don't make it to the top of the ladder because we don't try often enough. We're afraid of failure. In 1915 Ty Cobb set the record for stolen bases, 96. Seven years later, Max Carey of the Pittsburgh Pirates became second best with 51 stolen bases. Does this mean that Cobb was twice as good as Carey, his closet rival? Look at the facts: Cobb made 134 attempts, Carey, 53. Cobb failed 58 times; Carey only failed twice. Cobb succeeded 96 times, Carey only 51 times. Cobb's average was only 71 percent. Carey's average was 96 percent. Carey's average was much better than Cobb's. Cobb tried 81 more times than Carey. But here's the key: his 81 additional tries produced 44 more stolen bases. Cobb risked failure 81 more times in one season than his closest rival and Cobb goes down in history as the greatest base runner of all time. Why? Because Ty Cobb refused failure.

Babe Ruth hit 714 home runs. He struck out 1,330 times. If Ruth was in a batting slump, it never bothered him. He kept smiling, and he kept swinging the bat. During a low period an interviewer asked him, "How do you keep from being discouraged?" Ruth said, "I realize the law of averages will catch up if I just keep swinging. In fact, when I'm in a slump, I feel sorry for the pitcher because I know that sooner or later he's going to pay for it."

Keep Swinging the Bat

My nephew Eric was in his first Little League base-ball game three years ago. He was the youngest member of his team, so I went along to encourage him. It was Eric's first time at bat, and he was scared to death. Out on the mound was the biggest kid on the opposing team. The biggest kid is always the pitcher, and his name is always Butch. Sure enough, Butch threw that ball hard—strike one, strike two, strike three. Eric never got the bat off his shoulder. I could see how relieved Eric was when he struck out and got to go back to the dugout. But the coach was mad; he was hollering at Eric for not swinging the bat—forget not hitting the ball—and the fans were just going wild. I decided not to let this happen to one of my relatives, so I went over to him and said, "Eric, I don't know what this coach has told you, but let me tell you something. The object of this game is not to hit the ball. The object of the game is to swing the bat. Don't even try to hit the ball. Just go up there next time and swing the bat. Every time Butch pitches the ball, you take the bat and swing all three times, and I'll cheer for you."

Eric's turn came up again. This time the ball was already in the catcher's mitt before Eric realized it had gone by, but he swung the bat. I stood on my feet and yelled, "Great swing, great swing!" The rest of the fans kind of looked around at me as though I was a little odd. On the next pitch, Eric swung and missed. It didn't matter. "Great swing, great swing!" He struck out; I was on my feet cheering for him. He was so proud, because he did what he was supposed to do—swing the bat. So Eric was happy; I was happy. Margaret was at the game with me, and she was not happy. She thought that I was making a fool of myself, so she said, "I think I'll go to the car and read a book for a while."

I went over to Eric, tousled his hair, and said, "That was great. Next time Butch pitches, three swings again." He got up a little more confidence now, because all he had to do was swing the bat. Butch struck him out, and I gave him a standing ovation.

I knew that sometime during the Little League season, if Eric kept swinging the bat, the ball would eventually make contact with it. Sure enough, when Eric was up the fourth time, the ball accidentally hit the bat. I ran right alongside him to first base, cheering him on all the way. "Don't stop, Eric! Keep on going!" As Eric rounded third I was running alongside him again and we slid safely into home together.

Too many people stay in the dugout of life. They never swing a bat; they never face the challenge of a fastball or a curve. They may play manager, or be a batboy, but they never get into the game. Someday they're going to wonder why they never saw any action.

Now it could be depressing to think that life is passing you by—but here's the good news: **failure is not final**. So you never got into the game, or you tried and struck out? I strike out every day of my life—but that's OK. Get that bat off your shoulder and swing—give it the very best you've got, and then watch God make up the difference in your life.

Chapter Eleven

YOUR DECISION DETERMINES YOUR DESTINY

Today is a day of decisions—as is every other day of my life. In fact, I began the morning with the decision to get out of bed. My next decision, which apparently wasn't well thought out, was what I should wear. As I confidently stepped out of the bedroom to face the world, my 10-year-old Elizabeth took one look and said in her most gentle and loving way, "Dad, the tie is OK, but I think maybe you could have done better with the jacket." Ten minutes into the day and I had already made a wrong decision!

In this chapter I want to help you understand that decision-making is a process which, if practiced, will enable you to make better decisions for the glory of God. Joshua, in the well-known "choose you this day" passage, provides an excellent example of what goes into making right choices. As he is about to die, Joshua gives his farewell address to the people. First, he reviews the history of God's blessing the Children of Israel; then he says:

> Now, therefore, fear the Lord and serve Him in sincerity and truth; and put away the gods which your fathers served beyond the River and in Egypt,

and serve the Lord, choose for yourselves today whom you will serve: whether the gods which your fathers served which were beyond the River, or the gods of the Amorites in whose land you are living; but as for me and my house, we will serve the Lord. And the people answered and said..."We also will serve the Lord."
(Josh. 24:14-18)

We can draw several conclusions regarding decision-making from these few verses. *First, leaders bring people to a point of decision.* Joshua lead his people in the decision making process. As leaders, you and I are responsible for bringing our people to some needed decisions in their lives. Our journey through life is nothing but a process of decision making. As leaders, the better we are in bringing our people to right decisions, the more effective our leadership will be.

The second conclusion that we can draw from this portion of Scripture is this: *many things in life are decided for us and are therefore beyond our control.* Joshua realized this when he assumed that people, by nature, are subservient to someone. We have no choice. There are many other circumstances of life over which we have no control. We had no part in deciding whether or not the sun would rise this morning. We didn't decide to have a thunderstorm today. We didn't choose when, where, or to whom we would be born.

As we grow up and become independent, though, conclusion number three comes more and more into play: *there are many choices in life which we can make.* Joshua realized that his people could not choose *whether* they would serve, but they could choose whom they would serve. We can't always choose what our circumstances are, but we can choose what we'll do with them.

The fourth conclusion has to do with responsibility: *not only can we make right decisions*, we are responsible to *make the right decisions*. I find it interesting that as Joshua laid out the possible options for the Children of Israel, he made this statement: "Choose for yourselves." In other words, Joshua looked them right in the eye and told them they were responsible for their own decisions. He was saying, "I may be your leader; I may do my best to bring you to a point of decision; but the choice is still yours. You have to choose for yourselves."

The most important point I can make in this chapter and the most important one you can take away is that where you are today, in all probability, is a result of decisions you made yesterday. Until you take responsibility for your decision and resulting actions, you will always be looking for a scapegoat to blame for your problems. You and I are responsible for our choices. This is one of the most important lessons we can teach our children. When we have taught our children to accept responsibility for their decisions, to be able to say, "I was right" or, "I made a mistake," we have moved them to the head of the class in maturity.

Conclusion number five follows: *the sooner we make the right choices, the better*. Notice that Joshua said, "Choose for yourself *today*." He didn't add, "if you feel up to it" or "if it's convenient." Joshua knew that delaying a decision could lead to destruction.

Sixth, *leaders must decide first*. Often, as I observe a leader who is not moving his people forward, it becomes obvious that the leader is waiting for the followers to decide where they want to go next. This tactic never works. There is a reason, "It's lonely at the top." Someone has to stand in front of the crowd and make choices. A good leader has to be willing to stick his neck out and give direction.

Joshua did exactly that. He stood out from the crowd and declared unashamedly, "But as for me and my house, we will serve the Lord." He didn't know where his people were going to go, what direction they were to take. But he boldly declared where he was going. He knew that leaders make choices first; they don't wait for the people to decide what to do and then hop on the bandwagon with them.

Conclusion number seven is a corollary of number six: *the leader's choice influences other people.* If you are a successful leader, the moment you make your choice, people will follow, as in Joshua's case. Actually, this is the acid test of leadership. When you make a decision, do people follow?

Read verse 18 again: "We also will serve the Lord, for He is our God." Did you notice that word *also*? In effect, the people were saying, "We'll serve the Lord, because you're serving Him, Joshua." And verse 31 says, "And Israel served the Lord all the days of Joshua and all the days of the elders who survived Joshua, and had known all the deeds of the Lord which He had done for Israel." A tremendous amount of influence lies with the leader who recognizes the power of decision-making.

There is, of course, more to making a decision than saying, "Let's do it." In fact, the decision-making process is a complex one. But if you are to be a leader that people follow, it will be worth your while to understand this process. It involves five progressive phases. By way of illustration, I'm going to walk you through a major decision-making process in my own life—the call to come as senior pastor of Skyline Wesleyan Church.

Stage One: The Foundation Stage

Before you can make a wise decision, you need to understand the background of your situation. Why are your people where they are right now? Who made the decisions that led them there? It is impossible to jump into a situation and take control without ascertaining some historical information.

When Skyline's pastoral search committee called and asked if I would consider being a candidate, I answered yes. I was familiar with the church; my impressions were favorable. But there was a great deal I needed to know before committing myself. Returning home to Ohio from my first trip to meet with the search committee, I spent the entire time on the plane examining a large box of background information. I read year-end reports, financial statements, anything and everything that would help me better understand the church's history.

There were seven questions that I needed to answer and that you will need to answer before you have thoroughly worked through the foundation stage:

• *What is the track record?* Does the organization have a history of success or failure? Before I came to Skyline, I knew that it had a history of continued growth, godly leadership, and a good reputation in the community.

• *Who are (or were) the key players?* What kinds of people have been in leadership positions? At Skyline, Pastor Orval Butcher held the key leadership position, but other people and organizations were very influential. I came to find out that two groups in the church commanded the most respect: musicians and missionaries. Knowing this bit of information enabled me to know what was important to the people.

• *What has been their philosophy?* Has it been positive, progressive, visionary? Is it compatible with mine?

• *What is the organization pattern?* How is the structure run? Does the staff have control of the total operation, or do the lay people? One of the appealing things about Skyline was that is was (and continues to be) a staff-run church. I would never accept the senior pastorate of a church in which the lay people choose the staff.

• *What were the major problems?* As you examine the background of the situation in question, clearly identify what the main problems have been. I identified what I felt were two problem areas in Skyline's past. One involved a plateau period, a certain length of time during which the church did not grow. Another was that the staff was not strong in leadership. I've often joked with Pastor Butcher that if he were working with my staff, he would have church attendance running 5,000 now.

• *What were the major accomplishments?* What qualities stand out? I recognized that Skyline's major asset was the tremendous spirit of unity in the church body. The people had learned how to pull together. I knew that because of the love and warmth in the church, it would be easy to walk in and lead them.

• *What are the present goals and expectations?* It is often the case that your own goals and expectations are much different that those which other people have for you. And many times those under your leadership won't agree what their goals for you are.

After the pastoral search committee had grilled me for several hours, they began to draw the meeting to a close, satisfied that they had all the pertinent information. But I said, "Wait a minute! It's my turn to ask you guys some questions." They had found out what my goals were. Now I needed to know what their expectations of me were. "What do I have to do if I come to this church?" We all agreed that I would be expected to show up on Sundays and have a sermon ready. Besides that, the search committee expected me to build a great church. But then I discovered that there were a number of people who were counting on me to make home visits on a regular basis. Others expected me to perform all weddings and funerals. Not everybody's expectations of me were compatible. I had to evaluate their goals and my goals and then decide what was important.

If you are able to answer these seven questions about any leadership situation which calls for decisive action, you are on your way to making a wise choice. You have laid a solid foundation and are ready to move on.

Stage Two: The Fact Stage

At this point of the decision-making process you go on a fact-finding mission to help you better assess the situation as it really is. There are three key questions to ask at this stage:

What do I need to know? Before I came to Skyline, I needed to know what my job description would be. I needed to know exactly what I was responsible for and to whom I was accountable. I needed to know what my salary and benefits would be. These are the hard, cold facts of the job.

What do I know? After you have decided what facts you need to know, mentally check off the questions that you already have answered.

What do I not know? In my own situation, I knew what

the search would be expecting of me. I knew what they were going to pay me. I knew that they were behind me. I did not know, however, whether or not I would be so readily accepted by the congregation. I did not know where I would live or when my children would go to school. It can be difficult to make a decision when all the facts are not in.

Once you have answered these three questions to your satisfaction, you are in the position to make a decision, so make it. At this point, many people fall into the "what if ..." syndrome. These people rarely do anything decisive. What they need more than answers is a swift kick.

Stage Three: The Feedback Stage

At this phase of the process, you may get strong reactions. People will either confirm your decision or question your wisdom. This is a crucial time because emotions come into play. You will hear such comments as, "This is the way we've always done it!" or "But my grandpa helped build this church." Expect to take some heat after you have lit a fire.

The secret here is to develop an "inner circle." In my case, my inner circle is my staff. Your inner circle should be made up of people who are closely involved in your project, people who are knowledgeable, positive, and unintimidated.

How do you determine whose feedback is going to count? Let me give you six factors that should be taken into account:

Knowledge of the subject. Obviously, this is critical. If, for instance, I have to make a decision involving the music department, I am much more likely to listen to members of our music staff than our comptroller.

Skill. Not only should the person know the subject in question, he or she should be good at it. Our comptroller may have some knowledge in the field of music, but he can't carry a tune in a bucket.

Experience. This means successful experience, of course. There is no substitute for experience in giving a person expertise in any area. I am ready to listen to the person who has already lived through what I may be going through.

Responsibility. Someone who has successfully shouldered the responsibility of seeing a plan carried out will certainly have more credibility than a novice.

Strength of feeling. This is an intuitive thing, but when someone has strong feelings about an idea, it comes through. I love people of conviction. If a person is willing to lay his life on the line, he has my attention.

Principle. Am I well enough acquainted with the person to know that he runs his life on the same general principles that I do mine? If his principles are in violation of mine, he's not apt to be in my inner circle.

If a person qualifies in all six of these areas, he or she has my ear. If a staff member comes to my office to sell me a program and he passes all six tests, I'm in a position to buy.

The feedback stage is crucial in the decision-making process. If we don't spend enough time here, we're in danger of making the wrong decision. If we spend too much time here, we may never get the decision made. Actually, the greatest difficulty is not in knowing the right decision but in making it. After you know the facts, the history, and have feedback, you need to make your decision without delay.

Stage Four: The Focus Stage

At this point my attention turns from "What decision should I make?" to "How shall I make my decision work?" Here I move from the inner circle to the "outer circle." In this stage I need to focus on two concerns:

> PROBLEMS—What might torpedo the decision?

> PROCEDURES—How can the decision be effectively communicated?

I discussed handling difficulties in chapter 9, "Your Problem Is Not Your Problem," but here I want to give you a concise four-point outline for responding to problems:

> 1. *Anticipate them.* Don't let problems take you by surprise.

> 2. *List them.* Write down all the problems you're aware of.

> 3. *Address them.* Examine each problem thoroughly and think of a solution.

> 4. *Outsmart them.* If plan A doesn't work, be ready with plan B.

When we first began dealings to purchase land on which to relocate our sanctuary, the chairman of the relocation committee wrote to the congregation answering the potential questions and problems before they had a chance to ask. It kind of lets the wind out of a possible opponent's sail when he discovers you're one step ahead of him. Address the possible problem before it becomes a reality.

Once you have faced the issue and decided what to do about it, how do you proceed? There are five steps to take in order to make a decision effective:

>*Communication.* Make others aware that you're aware.

>*Consideration.* Enable your outer circle to visualize the positive results of your decision.

>*Comparison.* Evaluate your decision honestly. Compare the pros and cons.

>*Conviction.* This is the climax of the decision-making process. This is the step at which you reach a consensus.

>*Commitment.* Once you and your circle have agreed on the decision, they should stand with you in seeing that decision through to fruition.

Stage Five: The Forward Stage

This is the part of decision-making that I like: it's the time to move ahead. The critical element at this stage is timing; if your timing is off, all of your preparatory work may not save your decision. A good formula to remember regarding timing is this one:

>This wrong decision at the wrong time=disaster

>The wrong decision at the right time=a mistake

>The right decision at the wrong time=unaccceptance

The right decision at the right time=success

Now you have the five stages of decision-making. Don't underestimate the value of understanding and practicing this process. A leader's ability to make decisions and see them work means the difference between success and failure. Remember, success is not for the chosen few, but for the few who choose.

Chapter *Twelve*

I DON'T HAVE
TO SURVIVE

Survive—it's the most natural thing we do. We were born with an instinct to try to survive. We are born fighters.

But that natural desire to survive creates a conflict. In Galatians 2:20, Paul said, "I am crucified with Christ"—that's not survival. We're caught between resurrection and death. We all want the resurrection, but most of us don't want the crucifixion. This is a major problem in the church, both among church leaders and laymen.

What's the Problem?

The desire to survive keeps us at a mediocre level of living. It eats away at our conviction until we find it too easy to compromise and next to impossible to confront. The result of this survival mentality in the church is spiritual stagnation—maybe not death, but not exactly life either.

If our number one goal is to survive, we're no longer free to make the best decision. I find this all the time in leadership. We make decisions that are acceptable instead of making decisions that are right and godly. We take a poll as to what satisfies the people rather than what we know in our hearts is really right.

Also, if we desire to survive, we are encouraged to excuse our lack of effectiveness. We talk a lot about being faithful in the church; we talk very little about being fruitful. A fruitful person has to die first, so since most of us haven't died, we would rather talk about faithfulness. We may not really accomplish much, but at least we're consistent.

Another thing our desire to survive does is to sap our freedom and joy in the Lord. That's why there's a lot of talk in the Christian community today about burnout instead of move-out. We are trying so desperately to survive that we're operating in the flesh, and that is just wearing down our emotional and physical faculties.

Our desire to survive hinders us from completely obeying God. The Bible's heroes were characterized by wholehearted obedience. But if we are survivors, when it comes to the point in our walk with God where we may lose our skin, we cease walking in the light in order to preserve our flesh.

Our desire to survive robs us of the power and the blessings of God. When we strive for man's approval, that's about all we'll get. What we'll miss out on are the riches of God.

The Bible's Examples

There are a number of survival seekers in the Bible who, because of their desire to save themselves, lost the best that God had for them.

Lot is a good example. He chose the well-watered plains of Jordan. He took what was best for himself, and he lost his family in the deal. Ananias and Sapphira withheld from God what was rightly His and lost their lives because of it. King Saul wanted to keep his throne and his kingdom. He also wanted to keep all the glory to himself.

There's something common to all these people who tried to survive: they lost what they tried to keep. Whatever the survivor holds tightest he loses. It's a paradox evident in the teachings of Jesus. "Whoever wishes to save his live shall lose it, but whoever loses his life for My sake, he is the one who will save it" (Luke 9:24).

Sometimes we think that the people who have the most are the ones who hold on to it the tightest. The rich young ruler is a good example. But this is not necessarily the case. If you're a survival seeker, it's because of your mind-set, not your position or your possessions. Survivors have an "I want to stay alive at any cost" attitude. Anybody can adopt this philosophy of life.

How about Peter and his denial? There was a survival tactic if I've ever seen one. He tried to save his own skin. We could go on and on giving examples of those in God's Word who tried to survive. They paid a terrible price for their survivor mind-set. Solomon had an empty life; the rich ruler went away sadly after Jesus tried to minister to him; Peter will never forget the look on Jesus' face when He saw that His disciple had been unfaithful to Him.

The Bible also provides us with numerous examples of men and women who did not have to survive; they achieved great things for God because they were willing to put their lives on the line. Let's look at some examples here.

Shadrach, Meshach, and Abed-nego believed God would deliver them, but if He didn't, that was all right too. Caleb and Joshua came back with a different report from that of the other 10 spies, which again shows you that we are aren't compelled to strive for survival even in a survivor climate. They saw the same place, and they came back with an attitude that said, "Let's go possess that land!" David is another who didn't have to survive. The survivor would have said of the giant, Goliath, "He's so big he will hurt me." David said, "He's so big I can't miss."

How about Abraham sacrificing Isaac? Gideon didn't have to survive; he took just a few hundred men against thousands of Midianites. The widow with two mites was willing to give up all she had. She didn't have to survive. Again, it does not matter how much or how little you have; it's what percentage are you willing to give up? It is not a position in life. The widow gave everything that she had. The Apostle Paul is a classic example of one who didn't have to survive. We'll spend more time with him later.

"I Don't Have to Survive" Characteristics

Let me give you four characteristics of "I don't have to survive" people.

They have faith in God, not in themselves. They understand the value of placing their trust in God, because they recognize their own limitations.

They change people, nations, and generations. A leader who is willing to step out in faith may step out alone, but he will soon have followers. Together they will change lives. Many have changed the course of history.

They are willing to stand alone. A person who doesn't have to survive chooses to make the right decision even if it's not a popular one.

They possess unusual powers. God gives selfless people spiritual power. That's what makes the difference.

Some risk takers are getting a lot of attention in the world today—terrorists. This is certainly a negative example, but the terrorists provide a fitting example of what happens when somebody doesn't have to survive. The world doesn't know what to do with terrorists, because they do not care about surviving. We have no leverage on them. Even great powers like the United States are powerless against terrorists, because their lives are less important to them than their cause. They're willing to lay it all on the line.

Look at Israel's ability to keep their land even though surrounded by enemy nations. They know what it is to almost be extinct; they know what it is to face death, and they're willing to pay any price they have to pay to keep their freedom. They're a nation of people who don't have to survive.

We in the United States have enjoyed so many blessings for so long that we can't imagine being without them. We're not willing to risk loss because we have too much at stake. So we have become guardians of the goods, survivors to the end. We desperately need to shake off this mind-set.

Paul's Secret

I was reading Acts 20 one day, and I really think I found the secret to the Apostle Paul's life. Why was this guy so effective for the glory of God? On his way to Jerusalem, Paul met with the Ephesian elders and reviewed with them some of his ministry. "I did not shrink from declaring to you anything that was profitable, and teaching you publicly and from house to house...And now, behold, bound in spirit, I am on my way to Jerusalem, not knowing what will happen to me there, except that the Holy Spirit solemnly testifies to me in every city, saying that bonds and afflictions await me" (Acts 20:20, 22). Paul doesn't shrink from the message. He doesn't know what's going to happen except he knows it's going to be bad. He went on to say, "I do not consider my life of any account as dear to myself" (v. 24). This is a classic "I don't have to survive" statement. What mattered to the Apostle Paul was finishing the work God had for him. And he adds in verse 25, "I know that you all...will see my face no more."

No wonder Paul was such a change agent in the early church. No wonder he was willing to stand at the Jerusalem council and say that the Gospel was for the Gentiles as well as the Jews. No wonder he was willing to be the first missionary. The Apostle Paul didn't have to survive. No one could stop him. Those who didn't like some of the statements he was making on the council floor couldn't take away his position. Paul didn't have a position to lose. Those who wanted him to quit preaching could throw rocks at him, but that had happened before, and it didn't stop Paul. He would have counted it a privilege to suffer for Christ. They could threaten him with prison, but Paul could laugh and say, "Which one? Can I go back to Rome? I was witnessing there the last time I was in prison. Maybe I could help lead that guy to the Lord this time." Or they could threaten to kill him. "Would you? I have had such turmoil inwardly. I don't know whether I should stay with the saints or be present with the Lord; if you would just knock me off, that would take care of my dilemma." What could be done with the Apostle Paul? Absolutely nothing. Why did Paul choose to live this kind of life? So he could be independent? So he could call his own shots? No. He wanted to be crucified with Christ, knowing that in his own flesh he was powerless to preach the Gospel. And that should be our highest aim too. Only when we die to self can we live for Christ.

The Security Problem

One of the areas we are going to have to face is our insecurity. Insecure people are survivors; they're not willing to take risks, especially life-threatening risks. They have to have a second option; they have to have a plan B in their lives. They have a difficult time with failure. They tend to rely on things other than god. The person who doesn't have to survive says, "Here I stand; I can do nothing else. It's God and nothing else." The survivor says, "Well, it's God, but in case God doesn't come through, I have four other options to fall back on so I won't lose my hide." Paul writes in 1 Corinthians 4,

> Let a man regard us in the manner as servants of Christ....To me it is a very small thing that I should be examined by you, or by any human court; in fact, I do not even examine myself. I am conscious of nothing against myself, yet I am not by this acquitted; but the one who examines me is the Lord. (1 Cor. 4:1, 3-4)

Paul isn't saying he isn't going to submit to authority, but he is saying his security is not dependent on human decisions. He is saying, "I'm accountable to God."

What would happen if church leaders would be prophets instead of puppets? What would happen if we all became secure people who wait on the voice of God instead of insecure people who panic waiting on the voice of other people? This is not to say that the people don't matter. But if you can become secure in God, you will gain a freedom that people can never give you.

I grew up in a denomination where the greatest thing that could happen to a pastor was a unanimous vote from the congregation. When the pastors came together at district conference, all they talked about was their votes. I will never forget my first pastoral vote; the result was 31 yes, 1 no, and 1 blank. I remember getting on the phone in a panic, as a 22-year-old, calling my dad and saying, "Dad, should I stay at the church or not?" He said, "Well, what was your vote?" And I said, "Thirty-one said yes, one said no, and one didn't say anything at all. Is God telling me it's time for me to move one?" Dad just laughed and said, "John, that's a great vote. Quit worrying about it! Get on with it." That was probably the best vote that I ever had in my career. If my goal were to keep all the members of the congregation happy all the time, I would many times have to compromise my convictions, but I would more than likely get a 100 percent vote. There are times when, as a pastor, you need to listen to the voice of the people; it may be God's voice. But you should not be led by popular opinion; your sense of security should be anchored in the approval of God, not man.

The Success Problem

Another problem we have to face if we want to develop an "I don't have to survive" attitude is in the area of success. If we've had any success, we'll be tempted to guard it, to want people to continue thinking how wonderful we are. So we take fewer risks. We become a fortress instead of a moving army.

We build fences and walls around ourselves so that nobody can walk into our lives and destroy that which is so very precious to us.

Paul talks about the success problem in 1 Corinthians.

He says some very humbling things. "God has chosen the foolish things...the weak things...the base things...and the despised...the things that are not, that...no man should boast before God" (1 Cor. 1:27-29). In chapter 2 he writes that when he came to Corinth he chose to come to them in weakness and in fear and in trembling, not in persuasive words, but in demonstration of the spirit and of power (1 Cor. 2:1-4). One thing that the Apostle Paul says in this passage of Scripture is that we have a choice. Paul, though he was wise and brilliant, chose to come in weakness and fear. He could have come in and snowed them with all his languages. He could have come in and impressed them with the wealth of his knowledge and the breadth of his experiences. But he decided to put all that on the shelf and come talking about the cross of Jesus Christ. He decided to come in simplicity, not in profundity; in humility, not in arrogance.

One of the most important experiences of my life happened a few years ago when I was to speak at a large youth conference. For six months I told the church board to pray for me. I was sure this was going to affect many people. The organizers wanted a thousand young people to come forward and answer the call to full-time ministry, so I felt a tremendous responsibility. I prepared and prayed like I'd never prepared and prayed before in my life. Then in the Ramada Inn the afternoon of the evening I was going to speak, I sensed God saying, "Hey, John, by the way, I'm not going to use your message tonight." I don't get upset very often, but all of a sudden I realized that there were going to be 7,000 people there, and God was saying He wasn't going to use my message. I had worked a long time on that message. It was soul stirring, and those young people needed to hear it! But God said, "No, John. Listen to Me." I might as well have gotten on a plane and gone home.

But I stayed, trusting God had a better plan. He was impressing upon me that the success of the evening would depend on Him, not me. He directed me to read the passage in 1 Corinthians 1 and share with the kids that God was going to move mightily in the service because people had been praying. All He meant for me to do was to read the Scripture, pray, and give the invitation.

But I didn't do that. I read the passage, then I thought, *Well, I think it would help the Scripture a little bit to just use three or four great illustrations*, since I thought God needed me to bail Him out of this terrible problem. I told the first illustration and it bombed. I forgot the second one, so I finally just said, "Let's bow our heads." A wonderful peace came over me when I started to do what God had told me to do from the very beginning. Fifteen hundred kids came forward to say, "God has called me to preach in this service."

I'll be honest: when they came down that evening, I was both glad and sad. I was glad at what God was doing, but I was sad He didn't use me to do it. God was teaching me to stop worrying about my reputation, my success. He was telling me that if I'm to be successful for Him, He needs my listening ability, not my preaching ability.

If you're running in the reputation race, you need to decelerate and get off the track. I'd like to suggest five courses of action that will help you do this.

Don't take yourself too seriously.

We're constantly concerned about what other people are thinking of us, especially others who are running the race. When we begin taking God more seriously, we become less important; we can laugh at ourselves.

Create a climate of unqualified acceptance.

We need to create a climate where we accept each other just because we're brothers and sisters in the Lord Jesus Christ.

Fear God more than man.

We'll get out of this success syndrome and reputation race when we begin to recognize the frailty, the humanness, of man and the awesomeness of God. We will want to please God above all else.

Turn accomplishments into challenges.

Too often we rest on our accomplishments and don't take on any more challenges; we have too much to lose. What we ought to be doing is using those accomplishments as building blocks in the construction of God's kingdom, not pedestals to rest on.

Make room for innovators, entrepreneurs, to work.

We need to make room for people who don't fit the average mold, people who are daring enough to risk failure. We need to be their cheering section.

The Satisfaction Problem

In Revelation 3 we see that the church at Laodicea had the satisfaction problem. God said, "I know your deeds, that you are neither hot nor cold; I would that you were cold or hot. So because you are lukewarm, and neither hot nor cold, I will spit you out of My mouth...You say, 'I am rich, and have become wealthy, and have need of nothing,' and you do not know that you are wretched and miserable and poor and blind and naked" (Rev. 3:15-17).

When we feel satisfied with ourselves, we lack the compassion needed to reach out to others. It's hard to care for others when you don't understand the need. When we are satisfied and full, it's hard to help the people who are hungry and hurting. That's why Christians who have been in the church for a long time sometimes lack the compassion and desire to reach out to other people; they've forgotten what it was like to be out there. They have isolated themselves from the people who need to hear the message of the Gospel, the people who are still hurting and needy; they are no longer rubbing elbows with the crowd. Unfortunately, this is a real problem in the Christian community. Satisfaction has gripped the church. We have what we want and are happy with ourselves.

What are some characteristics of people who are in a state of satisfaction? First, they are unwilling to pay the price. They're unable to make right decisions. You show me a satisfied person or a satisfied church and I will show you one that is not able to make the right decisions, because the right decisions are the hard decisions, and the hard decisions are going to cost them something.

People in a satisfaction climate are more concerned about maintaining what they have than they are about meeting the needs of others around them. They have a maintenance mind-set. They want only to keep themselves happy. Their commitment in the church is not to the Great Commission at all but to clean rest rooms, neat bulletins, and potluck suppers. I see this in the denominations who have programs that are palatable to everyone, decisions that are accepted by everyone, plans approved by everyone, and progress witnessed by no one.

The Selfishness Problem

Another problem we have to deal with if we want to develop an "I don't have to survive" attitude is selfishness. One of the reasons people want to survive is that they want to be able to protect their rights. But if we want to be like Jesus, we have to give up our rights. Paul wrote,

Have this attitude in yourselves which was also in Christ Jesus, who, although He existed in the form of God, did not regard equality with God a thing to be grasped, but emptied Himself, taking the form of a bond-servant, and being made in the likeness of men. And being found in appearance as a man, He humbled Himself by becoming obedient to the point of death, even death on a cross. Therefore also God highly exalted Him. (Phil. 2:5-9)

I'm continually impressed when I think of the life of Jesus. He is the ultimate example for people who don't have to survive. He was in the robe of flesh, as we are; He had the same basic needs that we have; and no doubt He had moments in His life when He thought of surviving. The issue of survival confronted Him at the very beginning of His ministry, when He went to the wilderness and fasted for forty days. Satan came to tempt Him, to entice Him to survive. He offered bread for His body, a throne for an earthly kingdom, and the world bowing down before Him. Satan was setting Jesus up for survival.

It was before He began His great ministry that He was confronted with the issue of survival. Satan will use the same tactics on you. Before you accomplish anything great for God, I promise you, the issue of survival will arise in your life.

Jesus said some remarkable things about Himself.

- "The Son can do nothing of Himself, unless it is something He sees the Father doing." (John 5:19)

- "My judgment is just, because I seek not My own will, but the will of Him who sent Me." (John 5:30)

- "I do not receive glory from men." (John 5:41)

- "I have come down from heaven, not to do My own will, but the will of Him who sent Me." (John 6:38)

- "My teaching is not Mine, but His who sent Me." (John 7:16)

- "I have not come of Myself, but He who sent Me is true." (John 7:28)

- "When you lift up the Son of Man, then you will know that I am He, and I do nothing on My own initiative, but I speak these things as the Father hath taught Me." (John 8:28)

- "I do not speak on My own initiative, but the Father Himself who sent Me has given Me commandment, what to say, and what to speak." (John 12:49)

- "The words that I say to you I do not speak on My own initiative, but the Father abiding in Me does His works." (John 14:10)

Did you see all the *nots*? Not My words, not My teaching, not My judgment, not My deeds, but the Father's; not I but the Father; not My own glory, but the Father's.

How was Jesus able to cope with the pressures of His ministry? How was He able to minister to such a diverse group as the disciples? How was He able to have patience with them; how was He able to face the pressures of a crowd who wanted to put an earthly crown on His head? How was He able to withdraw from all those pressures and pray? Here's the reason: Jesus didn't have to survive. If I'm to be like Jesus, I too have to give up all my rights. You do too. The first step in "becoming of no reputation" and relinquishing our rights is in coming to the clear understanding that everything we are and everything we can ever hope to be can only be due to the power and grace of the Lord Jesus Christ. Could it be that we need a mission bigger than ourselves, a purpose beyond our limited vision?

Dying for a Greater Cause

In the first part of the fifteenth century a French peasant by the name of Joan of Arc was called to save her country from its enemies. Her sacred sword, her consecrated banner, and her belief in her mission helped her sweep away the armies that were before her. She sent a thrill of enthusiasm through the French army such as neither a king, a statesman, nor a president could produce. On one occasion she said to one of her generals, "I will lead the men over the wall." The general said, "Not a man will follow you." Joan of Arc replied, "I won't be looking back to see if they're following me." It was that kind of commitment that made Joan of Arc a national hero for the French. She was successful in delivering them from their English enemies, but she herself fell into English hands. As she was being burned at the stake, this 19-year-old was given a chance to recant; she was given a chance to betray her country; she was given a chance for liberty and freedom. But she chose the fire, and going to her death, she made this statement: "Every man gives his life for what he believes, and every woman gives her life for what she believes. Sometimes people believe in little or nothing, and yet they give their lives to that little or nothing. One life is all we have; we life it and it's gone. But...to live without belief is more terrible than dying, even more terrible than dying young." Joan of Arc had a purpose beyond herself; she didn't have to survive.

Let me give you the three characteristics of people who have been willing to die for a greater cause than themselves.

> *A purpose worth the price.* People who don't have to survive have a purpose that is worth the cost of their very lives.

> *A vision that is bigger than life.* They have the ability to see beyond their horizons. They are willing to make a sacrifice that they know will affect future generations.

> *A power that is greater than theirs.* People who don't have to survive aren't limited by their own weakness; they have a God-given power. Their purpose is God's purpose; their vision is God's vision; their power is God's power. His Spirit living in them makes the difference.

Chapter *Thirteen*

COMMITMENT IS
THE KEY

Back in the middle '70s, I reached a major decision-making period in my life. I was facing choices that would determine the course of my life and the effectiveness of my ministry. For over a year during that period I carried in my pocket a card, which I pulled out and read time and time again. After making my decision, I would waiver—and then reach for my card. I've read it hundreds of times. Because commitment is the key to success, I want to begin this chapter with the words that helped me in this area:

> Until I am committed, there is a hesitancy, a chance to draw back. But the moment I definitely commit myself, then God moves also, and a whole stream of events erupt. All manner of unforeseen incidents, meetings, persons, and material assistance which I could never have dreamed would come my way begin to flow toward me—the moment I make a commitment.

The greatest days of your life are the days when you sense your commitment to its highest degree. Your greatest days are not your days of leisure. Your greatest days are not even times when you have your closest friends around you. When something has seized you and caused you to have a high level of commitment to it, those are your greatest days. They may be your days of struggle, they may be your days of suffering, and they may be the days of your greatest battles in life, but they will be your greatest days.

If I could choose only one word to describe what's it's like to be committed, I think I would choose the word *alone*. If you become a person who is deeply committed to a cause, the world won't understand you; you will be alone. It's human to stand with the crowd; it's divine to stand alone. It's manlike to follow the people, to drift with the tide; it's godlike to follow principles, to stem the tide. It's natural to compromise conscience and follow social and religious fashions for the sake of gain and pleasure; it's divine to sacrifice fashions on the alter of truth and beauty. "No one supported me, but all deserted me" (2 Tim. 4:16). Those were the words of the battle-scarred Apostle Paul in describing his first appearance before Nero to answer for his life. Truth has been out of fashion since man changed his robe of fadeless light for a garment of faded leaves. Think about it for a moment.

Noah built the ark and voyaged alone except for his family. Abraham wandered and worshiped alone. Daniel dined and prayed alone. Elijah sacrificed and witnessed alone. Jeremiah prophesied and wept alone. Jesus loved and died alone. On His lonely way Jesus said to His disciples, "For the gate is small, and the way is narrow that leads to life, and few are those who find it" (Matt. 7:14).

Margaret and the kids and I went to the East Coast for a vacation last year. It was kind of a founding-and-forming-of-our-country vacation. It struck me that every historical site we visited was a monument to somebody's commitment in life. We went to New York City and saw the Statue of Liberty. There on Ellis Island stands the lady with her torch, the first thing so many immigrants saw in our country. I listened to guide talk about some of the things that happened to the immigrants when they landed at Ellis Island. They had such great hopes for life in America, yet they couldn't speak the language and didn't have a friend in the country. Sometimes they were detained on the small island for weeks or months; some died there. But many got to New York City and worked hard to carve out a place for themselves in this free society. That's commitment.

Then we got on a train for Philadelphia, a city rich in American history. As we sat in Constitution Hall, where the Declaration of Independence was signed, I realized the commitment level of our nation's founders. By signing their names to this document, these wealthy men were risking their lives and all they possessed. We also visited the graves of many of the signers, many of whom died penniless.

We went to Williamsburg, Virginia, where Patrick Henry began his leadership. He was the first American governor there, the man who said, "Give me liberty or give me death."

Two of the most impressive monuments we saw in Washington, D.C., the Washington Monument and the Lincoln Memorial, were built to honor the presidents who had the greatest struggles. One had the struggle of forming the nation, and the other had the struggle of keeping the nation. These are all monuments to commitment.

The World's Reactions to Commitment

In Scripture God gives us many great examples of committed men and women, with Shadrach, Meshach, and Abed-nego among them. King Nebuchadnezzar, the ruler of Babylon, has taken Israel captive and selected some of the promising young Hebrew men to be trained and serve in his court. Of course, the one known best is Daniel, but we're going to look especially at his three friends.

Nebuchadnezzar built a golden idol and instructed his people that at the sound of the music they were to bow down and worship this idol. It seemed that everybody was cooperating, but then some Chaldeans came to the king with an upsetting report: "There are certain Jews whom you have appointed over the administration of the province of Babylon, namely Shadrach, Meshach, and Abed-nego. These men, O king, have disregarded you; they do not serve your gods or worship the golden image which you have set up" (Dan. 3:12). The world reacts in several ways to people who are committed. The first response is brought out in this verse: the world takes notices of our commitment. These three guys really stood out.

"Then Nebuchadnezzar in rage and anger gave orders to bring Shadrach, Meshach, and Abed-nego; then these men were brought before the king" (Dan. 3:13). The second thing that happens is this: the world will be annoyed by our commitment. Nebuchadnezzar was downright mad; he flew into a rage. He couldn't handle somebody who didn't think the way he thought, believe the way he believed, or walk the way he walked.

"Nebuchadnezzar responded and said to them, 'Is it true, Shadrach Meshach, and Abed-nego, that you do not serve my gods or worship the golden image that I have set up?"" (Dan. 3:14) This verse brings our the next reaction: the world will question our commitment. Nebuchadnezzar had to double-check; he couldn't believe these guys had such strong backbones.

Nebuchadnezzar then said he would give them another chance to bow down to the image. "But if you will not worship, you will immediately be cast into the midst of a furnace of blazing fire; and what god is there who can deliver you out of my hands?" (Dan. 3:15) The fourth reaction is this: the world will test your commitment.

As those three Jews stood there that day, I imagine several thoughts went through their heads. They probably asked themselves questions like, Can God deliver us? What would it hurt if we bowed down just one time? I've often thought that would have been a convenient time for them to tie their shoelaces, so they could bow down; not to worship the idol, of course, just to tie their shoes.

When we come to the crossroad of our commitment the strength of our commitment has to prove itself. The choice will not be easy, because it's all or nothing. Our security, our identity, and our popularity may be at stake. It will not be a decision we can make lightly.

Characteristics of the Crossroad

When I'm at a crossroad of commitment in my life, a personal decision must be made. *Other* people may care; they may pray; they may offer advice; but the decision will be mine alone. I'm the one who will have to live with it and answer for it. Shadrach, Meshach, and Abed-nego stood together, but each had to make his own decision, his own commitment.

A second characteristic of a crossroad commitment is that *the decision will always cost something.* There is no such thing as a free commitment. In this situation commitment could have cost the Hebrews their lives. Your commitment may not be quite that expensive, but it will cost you something. It may cost you a friendship. It may cost you a few points in the popularity poll. But if it were free, it would also be worthless. Count on it costing.

A third thing I find at the crossroad is that others *will be influenced by it.* We never make a major decision at a crossroad without affecting other people. We may make the decision alone, and may walk the commitment alone, but we never make an important commitment that does not affect other people. It's like the rippling effect when a stone is thrown into a pond. The whole pond is affected.

Fourth, *it's the place where God reveals Himself to us.* Note that Nebuchadnezzar asked the men, "What god is there who can deliver you out of my hands?" Even the world realizes that our commitments are valid only because God intervenes.

A Right Concept of God

Our concept of God in crisis situations will determine our commitment. If we think God will fail us, flee, or be fickle, we'll never make strong commitments. We would be foolish to commit ourselves to someone who is irresponsible. But if our concept of God tells us He's sure, steadfast, true, and faithful, then we can make those commitments confidently.

Shadrach, Meshach, and Abed-nego were able to make the right kind of commitment because they had the right concept of God. They said to the king, "O Nebuchadnezzar, we do not need to give you an answer concerning this. If it be so, our God whom we serve is able to deliver us from the furnace of blazing fire; and He will deliver us out of your hand, O king" (Dan. 3:16-17). Their first concept of God was that He is able.

They went on to say, "But even if He does not, let it be known to you, O king, that we are not going to serve your gods or worship the golden image that you have set up" (Dan. 3:18). They understood that God expects us to do right regardless of the consequences. If we have that twofold concept of God, we have the glue for a very strong bonding for our commitment.

If we can begin to see God as one who expects us to do right regardless of the consequences, we won't waiver; God many times will bring healing and deliverance and power and anointing to our lives, but that's just the icing on the cake. Our concept of God makes a great difference.

Results of Commitment

What resulted from the commitment of Shadrach, Meshach, and Abed-nego?

> Then Nebuchadnezzar was filled with wrath, and his facial expression was altered toward Shadrach, Meshach, and Abed-nego. He answered by giving orders to heat the furnace seven times more than it was usually heated. And he commanded some valiant warriors who were in his army to tie up Shadrach, Meshach, and Abed-nego, in order to cast them into the furnace of blazing fire. Then these men were

tied up in their trousers, their coats, their caps and their other clothes, and were cast into the midst of the furnace of blazing fire. For this reason, because the king's command was urgent and the furnace had been made extremely hot, the flame of fire slew those men who carried up Shadrach, Meshach, and Abed-nego. But these three men, Shadrach, Meshach, and Abed-nego, fell into the midst of the furnace of blazing fire still tied up. (Dan. 3:19-23)

The first result of our commitment is that *we will be tried*. Bank on it: when we stand up for God, we will be tested.

The second result of our commitment is that *God will be glorified*. When are truly committed to Him, He will receive praise.

Nebuchadnezzar looked into the fiery furnace and asked, "Was it not three men we cast bound into the midst of the fire?" For he saw in the furnace four men, "loosed and walking about in the midst of the fire without harm, and the appearance of the fourth is like a son of the gods!" He called to Shadrach, Meshach, and Abed-nego to come out, and the three guys came out. In Daniel 3:27, we can see that the satraps, the prefects, the governors, and the king's high officials gathered around and saw that the fire had had no effect on their bodies. Their hair wasn't singed, their trousers weren't damaged, and they didn't even smell like fire. We can't even do that well if we go to a restaurant and sit in the nonsmoking section.

Nebuchadnezzar said, "Blessed be the God of Shadrach, Meshach, and Abed-nego, who has sent His angel and delivered His servants who put their trust in Him, violating the king's command, and yielded up their bodies so as not to serve or worship any god except their own God. Therefore I make a decree that any people, nation, or tongue that speaks anything offensive against the God of Shadrach, Meshach, and Abed-nego shall be torn limb from limb and their houses reduced to a rubbish heap, inasmuch as there is no other god who is able to deliver in this way" (Dan. 3:28-29).

How is the world going to know about the greatness of God without committed Christians? Our problem is not a lack of display of the power of God, the miracles of God, or the anointing of God; God is ready to do His part. He's just waiting for somebody to get into the furnace. He's looking for people who are totally committed, people whose purpose goes beyond their own abilities. There is a relationship between our willingness to die for God and His willingness to deliver us.

A third result of our commitment is that *God will bless our lives.* The king caused Shadrach, Meshach, and Abed-nego to prosper in the province of Babylon, according to Daniel 3:30.

Ordinary people can make an extraordinary impact on their own world. The secret lies in being totally committed to the cause of Jesus Christ. If you read the biographies of great men, you'll become convinced of a couple of things very quickly. One, all great men struggle; all great men have a fiery furnace in their lives. The second thing is that the degree of their commitment is what really make them great. They weren't smarter, they weren't faster, and they weren't better educated; they were more committed.

Developing Commitment

How do we develop commitment in our lives? From the story of Shadrach, Meshach, and Abed-nego, we can pull out several principles.

Commitment usually begins in an atmosphere of struggle. Very seldom do we see strong commitment arise out of a context of prosperity. Squandered time, wasted living, and distorted values may come out of prosperity, but commitment does not. The three Jews were captives in another land, with new customs, new surroundings, new values, and different priorities. It was for them an atmosphere of struggle.

Winston Churchill really achieved greatness during the struggle of World War II. His finest hour was the hour of confrontation, the hour of challenge. After the war he became an average prime minister, but not a great one. As Churchill was anticipating the fall of France in 1940, he said, "The battle of France is over; I expect the battle of Britain is about to begin. Upon this battle depends the survival of Christian civilization...Let us therefore brace ourselves to our duties and so bear ourselves that if the British Empire and its Commonwealth last for a thousand years, men will say, this was their finest hour."

Forty-five years later, nine out of ten people would probably say that Britain's finest hour came in the days of Churchill's leadership during World War II. Commitment usually begins in dark hours.

Commitment doesn't depend on abilities or gifts. Daniel, Shadrach, Meshach, and Abed-nego were among many good looking and intelligent youths chosen for special training, according to Daniel 1:3-4. But I like to think they weren't really chosen for those qualities. Rather, they were chosen because of their commitment.

Commitment is the result of choice; it's not a condition. People do not make great commitments because their conditions are right. People make great commitments because they choose to do right in spite of the conditions. In Daniel 1:8, it says, "But Daniel made up his mind."

The moment that Daniel made up his mind, the moment that Shadrach, Meshach, and Abed-nego made up their minds to serve God—that was their great moment. That's the moment God lifted them up. God blessed them because they chose commitment.

Commitment starts with the little things in our lives. No one ever made a big commitment without first making little commitments. It's a lot like learning to walk; we gain new confidence with each step. When we see that God blesses our small commitments, we begin to trust Him with bigger ones.

Don't make a commitment today to win your world for Jesus. That's idealistic and unreasonable. Make a commitment to win one person to Jesus. With the confidence you gain from winning that one, you can win two more.

Shadrach, Meshach, and Abed-nego started out on the right foot by refusing to eat the king's food. If you can't stand up and say no to the king's food, you can't stand up and say no to the king's idol. You don't all of a sudden get that kind of courage; it starts with the little things. You realize that when you said no to the king's food, God blessed you, and you prospered. If

God helped you on the food issue, He can help you on the idol issue. And step by step, we begin to build a foundation underneath us that gives us strong character for strong commitment.

This principle also works in reverse. Herein lies the danger of sinning: when you sin once, it's easier to sin twice. That's why we ought to have a healthy fear of temptation and a healthy fear of sin. Sin breaks down the walls of resistance. It causes our focus to become blurred, and all of a sudden we're doing things we shouldn't be doing. If you didn't make any strong commitments yesterday, it will catch up with you today.

Settle the issue of commitment before it arises. Don't get caught up in the emotion of the moment, because then your commitment will waver. Make your decision before the issue arises. The battle is won before the battle is begun. That's the secret behind the three Hebrews' success. They already knew what they were going to do. They didn't stand there and listen to the music and look at each other, wondering what to do. They had already settled the issue, so they didn't have to think about it.

Trust in God. In Daniel 3:28, after the Hebrews had been rescued and delivered, Nebuchadnezzar made an interesting statement. "Blessed be the God of Shadrach, Meshach, and Abed-nego, who has sent His angel and delivered His servants who put their trust in Him." Great commitments are built on trust in God.

Be single-minded. In Daniel 3:28, Nebuchadnezzar made another comment about these three guys. Not only did they trust in God, but he said they "yielded up their bodies so as not to serve or worship any other god except their own God." Single-mindedness.

In his book, *Choices*, Frederic Flach writes, "Most people can look back over the years and identify a time and place at which their lives changed significantly. Whether by accident or design, these are the moments when, because of a readiness within us, we are forced to seriously reappraise ourselves and the conditions under which we live to make certain choices that will affect the rest of our lives." We are never too old for that to happen.

There are some of you reading this book today, and you're thinking, *My Goodness, I've already been in this rut for twenty-five years!* Make some choices, make a commitment, take a risk—that's where the fruit it. It's never too late. Go for it! Don't allow circumstances or age or whatever to limit you. Only you can limit yourself.

In 1970 I read a book by Oswald Sanders, *Spiritual Leadership*. I became convinced after reading that book that the only people who are going to affect their world for God are those who become leaders and take a stand on principles that perhaps the rest of the world doesn't stand on. I can remember writing in the back of that book that regardless of the size of my congregation and regardless of the opinions of others—and I even wrote that regardless of what my father says, and my father is the greatest influence and the most important person in my life—there are some things I'm going to stand on and believe in. I'm still living off of that decision.

I was reading recently about John Wesley, a favorite hero of mine. He was writing a letter of encouragement to a fellow named George, who was leaving England to evangelize the new frontier. He wrote, "Dear George, the time has come for you to embark for America. I let you loose, George, on that great continent of America. Publish your message in the open face of the sun and do all the good that you can." I love Wesley's liberating phrase, "I let you loose."

Commitment will free you and let you loose to do great things for God.